BSA

Unit-Construction Twins

THE COMPLETE STORY

Matthew Vale

CROWOOD

First published in 2004 by
The Crowood Press Ltd
Ramsbury, Marlborough
Wiltshire SN8 2HR

www.crowood.com

British Library Cataloguing-in-Publication Data
A catalogue record for this book is available from the British Library.

ISBN 1 86126 689 8

Acknowledgements
The BSA unit twins were the top of the range bikes for BSA
throughout the 1960s and a large number were produced. Many of my
friends and acquaintances had owned them, and I was surprised when
on local runs to see how popular they still were. The idea for this book
was born when I realized how much information and how many
publications exist for the various incarnations of Triumph twins, and
how few address the BSA unit twins – again turning them into the
poor relation. Hopefully this book will help to redress that imbalance.

This book would not have been possible without the support of my
wife Julia and daughter Elizabeth, who have put up with me
disappearing to auto jumbles and runs with the excuse of 'I need more
information on this', or 'I need this part to finish that', or 'I must find a
196X model to photograph'.

Other major contributors to the project who have my thanks are the
past and present owners of examples of the model who were prepared
to let me interview them and photograph their machines: Chris Burrell
with his super 1972 Firebird; Jeremy Scott with his lovely 1962 Star;
and my brother, Nick, with his reminiscences of his 1972 Lightning and
just a single photo. Many thanks are due to Mick Walker, who was able
to supply a member of rare and hard-to-find images.

I also have to thank other friends and family for their support
throughout this project, including my mother Pat and my mate Tracy.

Finally, thanks are due to The Crowood Press for their commitment
to the project from its start, and their support and assistance during the
writing of this book.

Typeset by Textype, Cambridge

Printed and bound in Great Britain by CPI Bath

Contents

Introduction   4

1   The Origins of the BSA Unit Twins   5
2   Model Development   17
3   Technical Description and Development   66
4   Competition History   112
5   Owning and Riding Today   122
6   Twin True Stories   131
7   Restoration of a 1965 BSA A65 Lightning   147

Bibliography   173
Index   175

Introduction

Launched to the British public in January 1962, the BSA unit twin range still suffers from living under the limelight of its main competitors, the Triumph 500cc and 650cc twins. Even in the early years of the third millennium, Triumph unit twins of 500cc, 650cc and 750cc are more expensive and more in demand than the equivalent BSAs. The overwhelming popularity of the Triumph marque is reflected in the number of books devoted to the brand. Literature documenting the Triumph Bonneville, Trophy and Tiger models is common, but there are few books exclusively devoted to describing the BSA unit twins, despite their popularity at the time. Nevertheless, the BSA unit twin range, while never inspiring the loyalty given to the A7/A10 series, did have a dedicated group of customers, both here and in the USA, who appreciated the character, performance and charm of the range. This book sets out to redress the imbalance in the literature and to provide BSA owners and enthusiasts with a single source of information on the top of the range 1960s models.

Calling on the author's experiences, archive material, contemporary articles, road tests from UK and US motorcycle magazines, and current and past owners of the range, this book looks at the launch and subsequent development of the BSA A50 and A65, and charts the development, through a myriad of models, to the final, short-lived A70 and T65 of 1972. It also summarizes the competition history of the twins, looks at the experiences of running the bikes in the 1970s and today, and explores ways to improve them to provide safe and reliable transport on today's roads. To back up this information, the second half of the book documents a full restoration of an A50/65, showing the pitfalls and problems that can befall today's owner.

As the book charts the design and development of the BSA unit twins range, it also places these models in context against their greatest rivals, the Triumph twins. Paradoxically, at that time BSA wholly owned the Triumph Motorcycle Company, and was producing two directly competing product ranges for the whole ten years of production of the BSA twins. This must have been a contributory factor in the eventual failure of BSA, but that is another story.

1 The Origins of the BSA Unit Twins

A Brief History of BSA

Birmingham Small Arms, or BSA, was formed in the UK in 1861 by a group of companies involved in armaments manufacture, previously in an association called the Birmingham Small Arms Trade. The mandate of BSA was to 'manufacture guns by machinery' and a site for a factory was bought by the fledgling company at Small Heath, Birmingham. As the century drew on BSA was successful, but also recognized that the arms trade did depend heavily on the current government's policy and its response to the international situation, with massive orders for arms one year followed by none being the pattern. Often Small Heath would be working flat out for months to meet an urgent government arms order, then be forced to shut down once the order was completed.

To escape from this feast and famine cycle, BSA cast around for other products that could be produced using the machinery and capabilities it possessed, and so in 1880 started the manufacture of the Otto 'Dicycle'. This machine was a man-powered bicycle, but had its two wheels side by side with the rider sitting between them. Seeing the disadvantages of this layout, BSA soon started to produce its own design of the more conventional 'Safety Bicycle', which was the world's first rear-driven bicycle and established the fundamentals of bicycle design that are still current today. BSA continued to expand this side of the business to produce cycle hubs and other cycle components, which it supplied to other manufactories, becoming the dominant cycle component manufacturer of the time. In 1905, BSA started to look towards motorcycles as a logical step forwards from the production of pedal cycle components, and produced an experimental machine powered by a commercially available engine. The first machine, utilizing all 'in-house' components, was a 3½ horsepower single cylinder model, which was produced and put into production in 1910. From that date, BSA produced an ever-increasing range of motorcycles through the 1920s to the 1960s, with a model range that covered virtually every aspect of the market.

When the A50 and A65 model range was introduced, BSA and the British motorcycle industry were the dominant influences worldwide in the field of motorcycle design and manufacture, and the new models were intended to keep BSA there.

The Vertical Twin in Context

The 360-degree vertical twin was the definitive British motorcycle from the late 1930s when Edward Turner's 500cc Triumph Speed Twin first hit the road, and the A50 and A65 models were designed to follow the trend, rather than blaze a new path. Almost as light and slim as the singles that preceded it, but more powerful and smoother than them, the vertical twin was the right bike at the right time. All of the major British manufacturers rushed to get their own twins into production, and after World War II the Triumph was joined by 500cc four-stroke vertical twins from AJS, Ariel, BSA, Norton, Royal Enfield and Matchless. All of these first-generation twins were pre-unit, with a separate engine and gearbox (either supplied by a

The A65 and A50 models were produced on an up-to-date production line. This view of the line was taken in 1969.

Pictured at Birmingham's airport in 1964, this publicity shot shows one of the first BSA A65 Lightnings. Note the early style seat without the trademark 'hump' and the siamesed exhaust pipes with a single silencer.

specialized gearbox manufacture such as Burnham or made in-house), connected by a chain drive sitting in a chaincase containing the clutch that joined the engine and gearbox together – lots of joints and hence oil leaks.

Usually, these twins were originally 500cc, but were to grow and contract to provide various capacities, from 350cc through 600cc, 650cc, 700cc, 750cc and, finally, the Norton Commando at 828cc. It was generally accepted that the optimal engine size was 650cc, which gave an acceptable balance of performance, vibration and reliability. Larger capacities just had too much metal thrashing around, and most 750cc twins were in a softer state of tune than a fast 650cc. Norton, of course, got round the vibration problem on the Commando with its rubber mounting system (dubbed 'Isolastic', from 'isolate' and 'elastic', the two terms describing the characteristics of the system), but this really just masked the symptoms rather than fixing the problem.

Only BSA and Triumph produced a second generation of vertical twin engines, with the engine crankcases, chaincases and gearboxes all combined into a single set of (usually two) castings. The advantages of this system were many – fewer parts, hence the engines were lighter and cheaper, and fewer joints, hence fewer oil leaks and simpler maintenance. It also made for a more compact design, and enabled the power unit to be styled as a whole.

This engine configuration first appeared in a commercially successful form at the end of the 1950s with the Triumph 21 350cc model, and was adopted by both BSA and Triumph for their larger twins in the early 1960s. The BSA A50 and A65 unit twins formed the mainstay of the BSA range from the glory days of the British motorcycle industry in the early 1960s, through its decline and final demise in 1972. The range mirrored the fall of the British motorcycle industry, in that it was another refinement of a basic design that was revolutionary in the 1930s, but was already outdated when the first unit twin hit the road. It seemed that the creative spirit that had begun in the 1920s, and had taken the British motorcycle industry to its peak of

The original unit twin engine. Note the 'Star' emblem on the points cover and the single Monobloc carburettor.

engineering excellence in the 1950s, had died, and the best that could be achieved was to refine and develop what had gone before, rather than set a new trend.

Why Produce a New Range of Twins?

Despite their modern appearance, the A50 and A65 Stars represented an evolutionary procession from the A7 and A10 models that they replaced. BSA's first range of post-war twins was introduced in September 1946 as the 500cc A7, then extensively redesigned and relaunched as a 500cc (A7) and 650cc (A10) in 1949. By the launch of the A50 and the A65, the A7 and A10 range was showing its age, and finding it increasingly difficult to compete with more modern designs. Bob Fearon, then Director and General Manager of BSA, identified this as the reason for replacement in an interview given to Bob Currie in the old weekly magazine, *Motor Cycle*, in January 1962:

> Well, excellent as the old A10 Golden Flash undoubtedly was, it couldn't go on for ever. Even the most ardent BSA fan would jib at buying a new model that was virtually the same as his old one – and the one before that. Besides, by the time the A10

The forerunner to the unit twins was the A7/A10 pre-unit range. This picture is of an A10 Super Rocket, which was produced alongside the A65 Star in 1962.

approached middle age it had put on rather more weight than was good for it. Each succeeding development incorporated in the basic design had added to the weight.

A replacement was therefore needed – and Bert Perrigo, BSA's Chief Development Engineer, in the same interview gave an even more pressing reason for the change: 'We had to keep the USA in mind. In the American market the call is for something new, new, new all the time. It was becoming clear that extensive redesign was necessary, if interest in our product was to be maintained.'

So as a result of market forces, both at home and from the increasingly important US market, in

1960 BSA embarked on the design of a replacement for one of its most popular and profitable model ranges. The overall project was overseen by Bert Perrigo.

Another reason for the change was the cost and availability of electrical components. The A7/A10 range had 6V direct current (DC) dynamo charging systems, which only provided about 60W of power. While this was enough to power the 30W headlights of the time, it provided little spare capacity for the more powerful lights and additional electrical components that customers were beginning to demand. In addition, the dynamo needed an external mechanical drive to propel it, in the A7/A10's case a chain. A magneto provided the A7/A10 range with

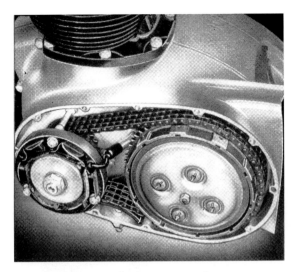

The Lucas alternator produced AC current and more power than the old dynamo it superseded. In the A65 it lived in the primary chaincase, along with the clutch.

ignition sparks, and although a magneto was efficient and reliable, it was also heavy, expensive and needed another drive, in this case a train of gears, adding yet more weight, complexity and expense to the engine. In the 1950s Lucas had designed an alternating current (AC) generator,

called an alternator, which comprised a static, six-coil stator and a magnetized rotating rotor.

This assembly was more powerful than the dynamo in terms of output; the one fitted to the A50 and A65 gave 60W initially, going up to 180W in the 1980s. The alternator was more reliable and lighter than a dynamo and, probably most important, was a lot cheaper to produce. In addition, it was designed to have the stator mounted in the primary chaincase and the rotor mounted on the crankshaft, removing the need for a separate drive. It also facilitated the adoption of points and coil ignition systems rather than using a magneto, due to the increased power output and reliability of battery charging. This enabled the deletion of both dynamo and magneto, and a corresponding reduction in cost, weight and complexity of the engine. The only downside of the system was the need to provide a rectifier to convert the AC to DC, but this component was relatively cheap and easy to produce.

The result of these factors was the introduction of two touring vertical twins, the 500cc A50 and the 650cc A65. Both were named simply 'Star' in the UK, and 'Royal Star' from 1963 in the US. These met the requirements

The A65 range initially comprised two models, the 500cc and 650cc Stars. This is the 650cc Star – identical in appearance to the 500cc model, apart from the larger front brake.

given above by being both lighter and less complex than the A7/A10 range by going to unit construction and using AC electrics and coil ignition. The layout of the engines did, however, follow that of the A7/A10 formula, as did the frame, but the new bikes were lighter and physically smaller than the current models – they weighed around 30lb (14kg) less and their wheelbase was some 2in (5cm) shorter.

When the Star was introduced in 1962, a reduced A7 and A10 range, comprising the more sporting models, was produced in parallel until 1963. The A10 range was finally superseded in 1964 by a full range of touring and sporting A50s and A65s. From then on, the A50 and A65 were to be the range leaders for BSA until the introduction of the A75 Rocket 3 three-cylinder model in 1969. However, the range never seemed to have the same charisma as its rivals, the Triumph 500cc and 650cc ranges. While the pricing of BSA and Triumph models was close, the number of Series B and C Triumphs produced was undeniably greater than that of the BSA. This disparity was due to the BSA being perceived (in the UK) as worthy rather than exciting. This was a major disadvantage, as motorcycling in the UK in the 1960s was changing from being an economic form of transport to a leisure-based industry – much as it had in the US ten to fifteen years earlier.

BSA Presents the A50 and A65 Star Twins

The BSA A50 and A65 Stars were introduced to the British public in 1962 in a bright and breezy yellow four-page brochure with the slogan: 'Twins! Two Star Attractions from BSA'. A pair of attractive twin sisters sitting aboard an A65 graced the cover, and pictures of the two new models with technical details were presented on the inside two pages.

The back page described the highlights of the models, including the triple-row primary chain, the 'graceful and compact' motor, floating-pad brake shoes and the mounting of the rocker spindles in the head. The brochure emphasized

both the forward- and backward-looking elements of the new model range's design, describing them as 'a unique blending of traditional, well-proved BSA features and innovations as modern as the centre of Birmingham itself'. All in all, it was very much in keeping with the period and reflected well the position that the models held in the BSA range of the day.

The launch was heralded in the contemporary motorcycle press, with *Motor Cycle* providing a launch report in January 1962, followed by an in-depth analysis of the A65 engine in February. At the time of the launch, the new models were recognized as being a major redesign of the previous A7/A10 range, and were described in the contemporary press as being 'completely fresh, but also following well-established BSA practice'. This could be viewed either as damming with faint praise, or as being aimed at reassuring the notoriously conservative British motorcyclist. It certainly echoed the 'forward- and backward-looking' description in the launch brochure.

The BSA design team had set out to produce an update of the existing machine, and only had two years in which to achieve it. They wanted a modern-looking machine, especially in the engine, but were unable or unwilling in the relatively short timescales to start with a completely clean sheet. The basic layout of the existing A7/A10 engine was retained, but with the gearbox incorporated in the same casting as the motor – hence the term unit construction and the retrospective description of 'pre-unit' for the separate engine and gearbox A7/A10 range. Adoption of the Lucas alternator in the primary drive side, and electrics including points and coil ignition in the timing side, meant that the outside appearance of the engine was cleaned up as there was no need for 'external' drives to a dynamo and magneto. The absence of external drives for the magneto and dynamo, plus the integrated gearbox, resulted in a smooth, oval bottom half, which was complemented by a very clean and tidy top end. All A50 and A65 cylinder heads were aluminium. Press reports in *Motor Cycle* also

The brochure that introduced the unit twins to the public was a delightful example of early 60s copy!

seemed to have coined the description 'power egg' for the engine/gearbox unit – it certainly retained no visual links to the A7/A10 – unlike the B-Series unit 650cc Triumph, the design of which almost seems to have gone out of its way to appear still to be a pre-unit. Possibly less complimentary but more descriptive was the application of the term 'watermelon motor' by US journalists of the day – although this seemed to be a term of affection rather than scorn. All in all, the press gave a very favourable reception to the modern, smooth engine unit.

In contrast to the modern engine styling, the running gear was very much a gentle evolution of the pre-unit twins style. However, this did not mean

that it was not up to date; indeed, the basic chassis was considered to be virtually state of the art for the early 1960s. It was certainly ahead of the then current 650cc Triumph frames in all areas except the admittedly subjective one of styling.

The frame was of steel tube all-welded construction, and was firmly based on the A7 unit. It had a wheelbase of 54in (137cm), 2in shorter than the A7/A10, thanks in main to the compact nature of the new engine. The swing-ing arm, in marked contrast to the Triumph efforts of the time, was adequately supported at the ends of its pivot rather than just the middle, and was also adequately gusseted, providing a rigid assembly. Girling units supplied the rear

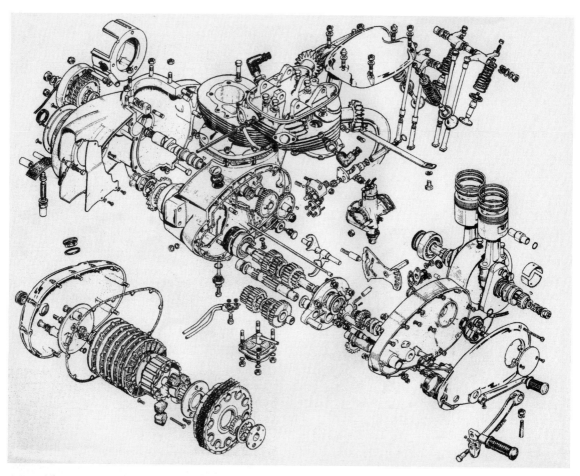

ABOVE: *The engine retained the layout of the A10 unit, but introduced unit construction. The gearbox was based on that fitted to the unit singles.*

The all-welded frame was a development of the A7/A10, with a shorter wheelbase. The original frame had a full loop rear sub-frame – this picture is of a 1965 A65 Lightning which had an 'open' rear sub-frame.

springing and damping, and the heavyweight BSA hydraulically damped fork was used, albeit initially with compression damping only. The wheels were 18in front and rear with full-width hubs, allowing straight spokes.

The rear wheel was common to both the A50 and A65, comprising a 7in diameter single leading shoe brake, initially cable operated, which was incorporated in a quickly detachable hub, retained by four studs and nuts. The A65 had an 8in front brake, which gave a good account of itself in contemporary road tests. The A50 in contrast had a 7in front brake, an interesting decision by BSA as the 500s had just as much weight as the 650s, and were only marginally slower. Presumably this decision was made to cut costs, as the A50 must have cost virtually the same as the A65 to produce. This brake was rightly criticized at the launch, and continued to be vilified in the press until 1964–65, when the factory started to fit the 8in unit to the 500cc range. With this one exception, the overall road holding and handling of the range was praised in contemporary road tests throughout the decade, although it was never mentioned in the same breath as Norton's featherbed frame.

The overall styling of the machine, in contrast to the modern-looking engine unit, was conventional BSA, with more than a passing nod to the A7/A10 range. The rubber-mounted 4gal (18l) petrol tank's styling was virtually identical to other bikes in the range, with the classic BSA pear-shaped badges contrasting with the chromed tank sides.

The pressed steel side panels were notable if not attractive, as they were very big, and completely enclosed the single carburettor. The objective was to move away from the 'bittiness' of previous styling and present an integrated whole. This objective was met, and styling was praised for this in the press. In the metal, there was very little space between the engine and the tank and side panels. The great British public was not so sure – to many eyes the overall styling was portly and it certainly lacked the lean eagerness that seemed to exude from a Triumph. The side panels emphasized the overweight appearance by looking disproportionately large compared to

The front hub on the original models was a full width cast iron affair. The design allowed for straight spokes to be used, giving strength and rigidity.

The large side panels completely hid the carburettor on the early models. The oval cover on the primary chaincase conceals the two clutch inspection caps.

The BSA heavyweight forks, although only one way damped were more than up to the job.

The nacelle carried the headlamp, speedometer, ammeter and switchgear. While neat, it offered limited and fiddly headlamp adjustment when compared with the later separate headlamp.

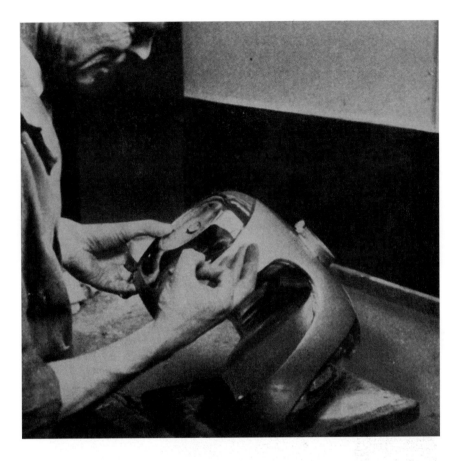

BSA in the mid 1960s was still keen to promote quality and craftsmanship. This photo from 1965 illustrates the hand lining of fuel tanks – to quote 'the lining of fuel tanks is one of the jobs where the machine has yet to be invented (even by BSA!) which can equal the superb skill of the man with a brush in his hand'.

the tank and engine. Mudguards had deep valances, again adding to the overweight and staid look of the machine. Ironically, the looks were deceptive, as the dry weight of both models was under 400lb (180kg), bringing them to within a few pounds of the B-Series 650 Triumph. Conversely, the C-series 500cc unit twin Triumph was substantially lighter than the A50, the 5TA weighing in at 341lb (155kg), against the A50's 385lb (175kg). There was a simple reason for this – the Triumph C-series 500cc twin was a bored-out 350cc, while the A50 was, in effect, a sleeved-down 650cc. In its defence the A50 did have the 650cc running gear (apart from that 7in front brake), so was a bigger and more robust bike than the Triumph.

The BSA corporate heavyweight front forks carried the headlamp and instruments in the second-generation BSA cylindrical nacelle. This was not as ugly as the one inflicted on the range during the 1950s, but was still not as good looking or stylish as the one on the Triumph Thunderbird.

Similarly to the Thunderbird, steel shrouds covered the front fork springs, which were in contrast to the sporty Triumph T110's rubber gaiters – but then this was typical British practice for what was deemed to be a 'tourer'. Sporty rubber gaiters and separate chromed headlamps would appear later, and eventually exposed chromed stanchions would be used in 1971–72.

Paintwork for the range at the launch comprised a black frame, nacelle and running gear with chromed wheel rims. The petrol tank featured pear-shaped chromed panels on each side, with the top and bottom painted. The side panels and mudguards were painted the same colour as the tank. For the first year of production these colours were Sapphire Blue for the A65 and

Polychromatic Green or Black for the A50, with an option of Flamboyant Red for the A65. In case this was too much frivolity for a BSA, sensible rubber knee grips were also provided on the tank for a refreshing touch of common sense. These had the dual role of protecting the chrome from a typical touring rider's waxed cotton over-trousers and providing a positive grip for the rider.

Overall, in comparison to today's razzmatazz of new model launches, the introduction of the A50/A65 range of models was low-key. The model range was made up of just two models, and these were the 'bread and butter' touring models. BSA seemed positively muted in publicizing the models, and the press, while endorsing the new designs, seemed rather matter of fact – the bikes were seen as evolutionary and slipped on to the scene with no fanfare – it was just business as usual.

2 Model Development

Introduction

Although the A50 and A65 were only in production for about ten years, there was (and indeed still is) a bewildering assortment of model names and designations. A further complication is the structure of the BSA product cycle – a sales season or year did not run from January to December, rather from August to July. So the 1965 season started after the works' summer holiday in August 1964, and ran through to July 1965. A '1965' model may therefore have been manufactured in 1964 or 1965. Confusing the registration date of machines with the manufacturing date further complicates

The A65 Lightning was the practical performance model in the range, without the out and performance of the Spitfire. This 1967 model year US model sports twin monoblocs and high bars.

By the mid 1960s, the market had changed, and motorbikes were seen as leisure vehicles. This US market Spitfire Mk IV appeared in the 1968 brochure.

The 1968–69 Remarking of Models

The 1967–68 selling season in the USA was not good for BSA, and there were substantial numbers of unsold bikes, rumoured to be around 1,800 either returned from the US unused, or that were stored at the UK docks for shipping but never dispatched. This represented a considerable cost to the factory. The reasons for this appeared to be that BSA production targets had not been met, resulting in the time-sensitive US selling market being missed – most of the US sales were concentrated in the initial few months of a year, so woe betide the manufacturer who did not get his goods on the dealers' floors for that time. This resulted in the returned US market 1967–68 model year bikes being updated to the following year's specification by the factory and being sold in the UK and back in the US through the factory dealerships as 1969–70 models. While the bikes were updated in appearance to the later specification, including brakes and colours, the basic engine and frame remained unchanged, as did the frame and engine numbers. This, of course, helps to contribute to the confusion that surrounds the age of some bikes – while they may have been first registered in the UK or the US during 1970, the bike itself may well be a year or more older.

the issue. Often, 'previous' year's models were not all sold and would be first registered after the new season's models had been released. So the happy but possibly uninformed owner could claim rightly that his 1965 model Lightning was a 1966 model because that was the year when he bought it. To add to the confusion, some models were introduced during a notional model year – the original A50 and A65 Stars were introduced to the UK market in January 1962. In the descriptions of models that follow, any reference to a year is referring to a model year, so 1965 means August 1964 through to July 1965. Finally, the reader should bear in mind that the introduction of the models in January 1962 was in fact halfway through the 1962 model year.

The spread of models offered to the buying public can be broadly divided up in two ways: by capacity – 500cc and 650cc; and function – touring, sporting and off-road. The evolution of both sizes of machine followed the same path – incremental development of more and more powerful models. The A50 range, however, had fewer models than the A65 and to a certain extent can be considered to be the poor relation of the range. The tables on pages 20 and 31 give an overview of the models in the ranges by year. They include details of the particular model designations as stamped on the engines and frames. It should be noted that up to the 1966 model year, engines and frames did not carry the same number or codes. Numbers were the same from the 1966 model year, and codes were standardized from the 1967 model year. So a 1965 or earlier A50 or A65 with matching engine and frame numbers should be viewed with suspicion, because it is pretty unlikely that

it left the factory like that! Also, up until the 1967 model year, all frames followed the BSA standard of a single prefix (in this case A50) to identify the frame in a range. The frame prefix was sometimes followed by a code to denote specific models in the range. Engine prefixes denoted the capacity (A50 and A65) and were, like the frame prefix, sometimes followed by a model identifier code.

The United States of America was a major export market for BSA, increasing in importance throughout the 1960s. This influence is shown in the styling and detail fitting of the unit twins, with the early models being easily distinguishable between the US and UK and general export models. The US models adopted sports styling, mudguards and small tanks from the word go, and, as the decade progressed, these features were incorporated on to the home-market products to rationalize production and spares inventories.

Towards the end of the decade, apart from US-market-only models such as the Firebird, the main difference between UK and US Thunderbolt and Lightning models was the size of the fuel tank – and even then the styling was very similar! The

This is the first A50. Finished in Polychromatic Green and Black, with the option of all Black, it was a steady rather than startling concoction.

oil-in-frame models for the US and the UK for 1971 were to all intents and purposes identical, again apart from the fuel tank size and styling.

The A50 Range

The table below provides a summary of the A50 range, identifying the model codes, names, engine and frame prefixes and the model year(s) in which the particular models were offered.

A50 Star Twin: 1962–65

The A50 Star Twin was used as a model name in the UK from the model's introduction in 1962 through until the 1966 model year. This was the touring version of the A50, and throughout its life was supplied with a single 1in bore Amal Monobloc carburettor, soft state of tune, large

valances to the mudguards, and steel side panels that enclosed the carburettor and the headlamp in a nacelle that also held the speedometer and switches. It was available as standard in a Polychromatic Green finish for the tank, side panels and mudguards, with black enamelled frame, forks and nacelle, with an alternative colour of plain Black. The tank had the BSA trademark chromed side panels, with the red and gold pear-shaped badges.

With a bore and stroke of 65.5mm by 74mm, a compression ratio of 7.5:1 (0.25 higher than that of the A65 Star), a 1in choke Monobloc and a standard cam, the performance was adequate rather than startling. In fact, the compression ratio was raised midway through 1962 to 8:1 to improve performance. BSA obviously thought the performance was more than adequate,

BSA A50 Model Designations and Years

Model Code	Model Name	Engine and Frame Codes		Model Year – August to July										
		Frame Prefix	Engine Prefix	61–62	62–63	63–64	64–65	65–66	66–67	67–68	68–69	69–70	70–71	71–72
A50	Star Twin (cable rear brake)	A50	A50	★										
A50	Star Twin (rod rear brake)	A50A	A50	★										
A50	Star/Royal Star (rod or cable brake)	A50	A50		★									
A50R	Star/Royal Star	A50	A50A			★	★							
A50	Police	A50	A50AP			★	★							
A50C	Cyclone (road model)	A50B	A50D				★							
A50CC	Cyclone Competition	A50B	A50D				★							
A50R	Royal Star	A50C	A50R					★						
A50W	Wasp	A50C	A50W					★						
A50R	Royal Star	A50RA							★					
A50W	Wasp	A50WA							★					
A50R	Royal Star	A50RB								★				
A50W	Wasp	A50WB								★				
A50R	Royal Star	A50R										★	★	

Note that from the 1964–67 model years the letter 'C' after engine designation (for example, A50BC) indicated factory fitment of a close ratio gearbox however, to quote from the launch brochure: 'Both 500 and 650 power units are packed with biting performance which can be kid-gloved at will into superbly quiet and docile masterpieces, installed in robust BSA duplex full cradle frames, and equipped with braking power to match.'

The main change made to the Star in its life cycle was the replacement of the 7in front brake with the A65 Star's 8in unit for the final 1964–65 model year; otherwise, the model changed little during its 3½-year life. The Star was replaced in the UK by the Royal Star for the 1966 model year.

A50 Royal Star: 1962–70

The Royal Star name was used for the 500cc US models from 1962, and was used to designate UK models from 1966. The early US models were the same as the UK Star models with the exception of the usual US model changes of higher handlebars, passenger grab rail on the dual seat, and a smaller fuel tank, carrying only 3gal (13.6l) of petrol and without the UK's chrome trim strip across the top. The Royal Star continued in the Star's role as the tourer of the range (the term 'entry level' not having been coined at that time!), and basically was continued with no innovative changes – the model tended to adopt the changes and improvements shown by the more 'glamorous' models in the range some time after they first appeared. For example, the nacelle was replaced by a separate chromed headlamp in 1966 and fork-yoke-mounted speedometer only in 1966, a full year after they were introduced on the Cyclone. Carburettors fitted started off with the 1in bore Amal Monobloc at the launch, eventually moving to a single Amal Concentric of 26mm bore for the Royal Star of 1968 – again the upgrade of carburettor type lagging a year behind the 650cc sports models.

The 1966 Royal Star shared the open-ended rear sub-frame with the other models in the range, and while its engine remained a softly tuned unit with a single carburettor, the cycle parts were brought into line with the appearance and specification of the rest of the range. The original full-width front and rear wheels were

Despite introducing the Lightning and having the Rocket, BSA still place an image of the Star on the front of their 1965 model year brochure.

changed to those on the sporting models in the range, and the brakes were changed to the half-width 8in front and 7in rear – bringing parity with the 650cc models at last. It lost the nacelle, and was equipped with the new two-way damped front forks, which also substituted rubber gaiters for the original front fork metal spring shrouds. A separate headlamp with a

A50 Star Specifications			
1961–3/1963–4/1964–5	**A50 Star (1961–3)**	**A50 Star (1963–4)**	**A50 Star (1964–5)**
Engine			
Compression ratio	7.50:1 (mid 62 – 8.0:1)	8.50:1	8.50:1
Ignition	Coil	Coil	Coil
Bore & stroke	65.5 × 74mm	65.5 × 74mm	65.5 × 74mm
Carburettor			Single
Type (Amal)	Monobloc	Monobloc	Monobloc
Size	1in	1in	1in
Transmission – sprockets			
Engine	28	28	28
Clutch	58	58	58
Gearbox (solo)	17	17	17
Gearbox (sidecar)	16	16	16
Rear wheel (solo)	42	42	42
Rear wheel (sidecar)	43	43	43
Gearing			
Top gear (solo)	5.12	5.11	5.12
Third gear (solo)	6.04	5.85	5.85
Second gear (solo)	8.44	8.18	8.18
First gear (solo)	13.1	12.82	12.82
Brakes			
Front (diameter)	7in	7in	8in
Front hub	Cast iron, full-width	Cast iron, full-width	Cast iron, full-width
Rear (diameter)	7in	7in	7in
Rear hub	Cast iron, full-width	Cast iron, full-width	Cast iron, full-width
Tyres			
Front (size)	3.25 × 18	3.25 × 18	3.25 × 18
Front (type)	Ribbed	Ribbed	Ribbed
Rear (size)	3.50 × 18	3.50 × 18	3.50 × 18
Rear (type)	Universal	Gold Seal	Gold Seal
Electrics			
Voltage	6V	6V	6 (12V option)
Headlamp size	7in	7in	7in
Weights and capacities			
Fuel tank	4gal (18l)	4gal (18l)	4gal (18l)
Oil tank	6pt (3.3l)	5½pt (3.1l)	5½pt (3.1l)
Seat height	31½in (80cm)	30½in (77.5cm)	30½in (77.5cm)
Length	81in (206cm)	81in (206cm)	81in (206cm)
Wheelbase	54½in (138.5cm)	54½in (138.5cm)	54½in (138.5cm)
Width	28in (71cm)	28in (71cm)	28in (71cm)
Ground clearance	7in (17.8cm)	7in (17.8cm)	7in (17.8cm)
Weight	385lb (175kg)	385lb (175kg)	385lb (175kg)

The 1966 Royal Star had lost the Star's nacelle, but retained the carburettor-enclosing side panels. The valanced rear and slimmer front mudguards were painted.

By 1968 the US-market Royal Star was looking sportier, with slim mudguards and a small tank. However, there was no tachometer and the guards were painted.

chrome shell was mounted on brackets on the front forks, and slimmer mudguards were fitted front and rear. A speedometer was mounted on the fork top yoke. The compression ratio was raised to 9.0:1. These modifications gave a much more sporty appearance to the A50, and also provided some practical improvements to the handling and performance. It could be argued that the model's utility was reduced, largely due to the less efficient mudguards and slightly peakier performance, but overall the changes gave a much more attractive and modern appearance, with performance to match.

The Royal Star then was produced in this form until 1970 with few changes – probably the most noticeable being the change to a hump-back seat in 1967. The Royal Star was the last of the A50 models to be produced, with the off-road Wasp being discontinued for the 1968–69 model year, and was discontinued before it could benefit from the new oil-in-frame running gear of the 1971 model year.

A50 Cyclone, Cyclone Competition and Cyclone Clubman: 1964–65

The Cyclone was the first sports incarnation of the A50, and featured in both on and off-road incarnations. The A50CC Cyclone Competition model was introduced in 1964 in the US as an off-road scrambler. Tested in *Cycle World* it was described as 'having all the sturdiness and thunderous power that made the old single [the 500cc Gold Star] a winner'.

Essentially a tuned-up and stripped-down A50, the Cyclone had a 9:1 compression ratio, twin 1$\frac{1}{16}$in Amal Monobloc carburettors, hot camshafts, large tyres (3.25×19 front, 4.00×18 rear), blade type mudguards, upswept exhaust pipes with no silencers, and no instruments, lights or side panels. The inlet valves of the 1965 Cyclone were increased in size to 1.45in – 0.04in larger than those fitted to the standard A50. The 8in half width brake was fitted to the front, with the QD (quickly detachable) 7in half-width hub at the rear, and wheels were 19in front and rear, fitted

The last year for the Royal Star was 1970. By then it had acquired the TLS front brake, but was otherwise little changed in appearance from the 1968 model.

A50 Royal Star Specifications

	A50 Royal Star (1965–6)	A50 Royal Star (1966–7)	A50 Royal Star (1967–8)	A50 Royal Star (1968–9)	A50 Royal Star (1969–70)
Engine					
Compression ratio	9.0:1	9.0:1	9.0:1	9.0:1	9.0:1
Ignition	Coil	Coil	Coil	Coil	Coil
Bore & stroke	65.5 × 74mm	65.5 × 74mm	65.5 × 74mm	65.5 × 74mm	65.5 × 74mm
Carburettor					
Number	Single	Single	Single	Single	Single
Type (Amal)	Monobloc	Monobloc	Concentric	Concentric	Concentric
Size	1in	1in	26mm	26mm	26mm
Transmission – sprockets					
Engine	28	28	28	28	28
Clutch	58	58	58	58	58
Gearbox (solo)	18	18	18	18	18
Rear wheel (solo)	47	52	47	47	47
Gearing					
Top gear (solo)	5.41	5.41	5.41	5.41	5.41
Third gear (solo)	6.2	6.2	6.2	6.2	6.2
Second gear (solo)	8.67	8.67	8.67	8.67	8.67
First gear (solo)	13.6	13.6	13.6	13.6	13.6
Brakes					
Front	8in	8in	8in	8in TLS	8in TLS
Front hub	Half-width	Half-width	Half-width	Full-width	Full-width
Rear	7in	7in	7in	7in	7in
Rear hub	Half-width, QD	Half-width, QD	Half-width, QD	Half-width, QD	Half-width, QD
Tyres					
Front (size)	3.25 × 19	3.25 × 19	3.25 × 19	3.25 × 19	3.25 × 19
Front (type)	Ribbed	Ribbed	K70	K70	K70
Rear (size)	3.50 × 19	4.00 × 18	4.00 × 18	4.00 × 18	4.00 × 18
Rear (type)	K70	K70	K70	K70	K70
Electrics					
Voltage	12V	12V	12V	12V	12V
Headlamp size	7in	7in	7in	7in	7in
Weights and capacities					
Fuel tank	4gal (18l)	3½gal (16l)	3½gal (16l)	4gal (18l)	4gal (18l)
Oil tank	5½pt (3.1l)	5pt (3l)	5pt (3l)	5pt (3l)	5pt (3l)
Seat height	31½in (80cm)	31½in (80cm)	32in (81.3cm)	32in (81.3cm)	32in (81.3cm)
Length	85½in (216cm)	85½in (216cm)	85½in (216cm)	85½in (216cm)	85½in (216cm)
Wheelbase	56in (142cm)	56in (142cm)	56in (142cm)	56in (142cm)	56in (142cm)
Width	28in (71cm)	28in (71cm)	28in (71cm)	28in (71cm)	28in (71cm)
Ground clearance	8in (20cm)	8in (20cm)	8in (20cm)	7½in (19cm)	7½in (19cm)
Weight	391lb (18kg)	391lb (178kg)	408lb (185kg)	383lb (179kg)	402lb (182kg)

This Rocket or Cyclone sports the chromed mudguards and headlamp that marked the model's change from the touring 'Star' to an altogether more sporting machine.

A one-year wonder, the 1965 road-going Cyclone was identical in appearance to the Lightning. At least it had a tachometer as standard.

A50 Cyclone Specifications

	A50 Cyclone (1964–5)
Compression ratio	9.0:1
Ignition	Coil
Bore & stroke	65.5 × 74mm
Carburettor	
Number	Twin
Type (Amal)	Monobloc
Size (in)	1¹⁄₁₆in
Transmission – sprockets	
Engine	28
Clutch	58
Gearbox (solo)	17
Gearbox (sidecar)	–
Rear wheel (solo)	42
Rear wheel (sidecar)	–
Gearing	
Top gear (solo)	5.12
Third gear (solo)	5.85
Second gear (solo)	7.56
First gear (solo)	10.39
Brakes	
Front (diameter)	8in
Front hub	Half-width
Rear (diameter)	7in
Rear hub	Half-width, QD
Tyres	
Front (size)	3.25 × 19
Front (type)	Ribbed
Rear (size)	3.50 × 19
Rear (type)	Gold Seal
Electrics	
Voltage	6 (12V option)
Headlamp size	7in
Weights and capacities	
Fuel tank	4gal (18l)
Oil tank	5½pt (3.1l)
Seat height	3in (79cm)
Length	85in (215cm)
Wheelbase	56in (142cm)
Width	27in (68.6cm)
Ground clearance	7½in (19m)
Weight	398lb (180.5kg)

Notes: Specification of the A50 Cyclone is for the UK-market road version.

with 3.25 section front and 4.00 section rear tyres. Curb weight was quoted in the *Cycle World* test as 384lb (174kg), as against the 406lb (184kg) quoted for the Royal Star, which the magazine tested in 1962. The petrol tank was shared with the US Lightning Rocket and Cyclone Road model, bearing round type BSA badges similar to those fitted to the original BSA Gold Star. Accompanying the Competition model in the US was the road version – the A50C Cyclone which shared the modifications outlined above, but included full road lighting gear and instruments.

However, when the Cyclone was introduced on to the British market for the 1965 model year, it was positioned alongside the Lightning as a high-performance twin for the road.

Specification of the 1965 UK Cyclone was as per the 1965 Lightning, with full road equipment including lights and battery, standard 12V battery and coil ignition system (although it is possible that early models may be 6V), rather than the energy transfer system, low-level siamesed exhaust pipes and single silencer, twin Amal Monobloc carburettors, and 3.25×19 front and 3.50×19 rear tyres. The compression ratio was 9.0:1, which, along with the twin carburettors, gave it a power boost over the standard A50 Star. The standard petrol tank, with pear-shaped badges and chrome panels, was fitted. BSA quoted the weight of the UK Cyclone, with all its road equipment as 398lb (180kg) – exactly the same weight as the 650cc Lightning. BSA also offered the Cyclone Clubman, a lightly modified bike for production racing.

Changes from the standard Cyclone comprised rear-set footrests and foot controls, racing seat, sports silencer and dropped handlebars – the same as the Lightning Clubman. The Cyclone was replaced in both the UK and US markets in 1966 by the Wasp.

A50 Wasp: 1966

The Wasp was produced only in the 1966 model year, although some sources also indicate that production extended into the 1967 model year – however, the 1967 BSA brochures for the UK and the USA do not list the model. However,

The Cyclone Clubman was a production racer version of the 500cc bike. The model sported ace bars, rearsets and a racing-style seat.

The 1966 model Wasp took over from the off-road Cyclone, and again had no lights. This year saw the first appearance of the smart 2gal (9l) glass-fibre tank that was shared with the Hornet and Spitfire models.

the 650cc Hornet was listed for the 1967 model year in the USA. The Wasp was a purely off-road machine – aimed at the US race tracks of the time. There was no equivalent road-going model marketed in the UK. Presumably this meant that the previous year's Cyclone and Cyclone Competition models did not sell well in the UK.

The Wasp was a development of the US market Cyclone, and was a pure off-road racer. BSA described it as a scaled-down Hornet – which was promoted as a closed circuit racer. The engine was broadly as the previous year's Cyclone, with twin Amal Monobloc carburettors and a higher state of tune than the 'cooking' Royal Star. The compression ratio was up to 10.5:1. However, in contrast to the Cyclone, the Wasp had twin downswept exhaust pipes with silencers, and introduced the small 2gal (9l) glass-fibre petrol tank, also used on the Spitfire Mk II. Ignition was provided by the energy transfer system, which removed the need for the battery, and along with the Hornet remained at 6V. Instrumentation comprised speedometer and tachometer, and no lights were fitted, although the rear number plate carrier was. Cutaway glass fibre side panels were specified. The model was fitted with the new-for-1966 two-way damped front forks, with rubber gaiters and plain chromed tubes rather than the 'eared' headlamp brackets that covered the stanchions between the top and bottom yokes. Slim chromed mudguards were fitted. Wheels were 19in front and 18in rear, and were shod with Dunlop K70 tyres. The tyres were the widest fitted to the range in 1966, with a 3.50 section front and 4.00 section rear, the same as the Hornet. Brakes were the 8in single-sided front and the 7in rear on the later quickly detachable hub.

The Wasp was the last of the high-performance 500cc models. Once it was dropped from the range, only the Royal Star in the UK and the USA represented the A50 range.

The A65 Range

The following table provides a summary of the A65 range, identifying the model codes, names, engine and frame prefixes and the model year(s)

A50 Wasp Specifications

	A50 Wasp (1965–6)
Engine	
Compression ratio	10.5:1
Ignition	Energy transfer
Bore & stroke	65.5 × 74mm
Carburettor	
Number	Twin
Type (Amal)	Monobloc
Size	1⅛in
Transmission – sprockets	
Engine	28
Clutch	58
Gearbox (solo)	18
Rear wheel (solo)	47
Gearing	
Top gear (solo)	5.41
Third gear (solo)	6.2
Second gear (solo)	8.67
First gear (solo)	13.6
Brakes	
Front	8in
Front hub	Half-width
Rear	7in
Rear hub	Half-width, QD
Tyres	
Front (size)	3.50 × 19
Front (type)	K70
Rear (size)	4.00 × 18
Rear (type)	K70
Electrics	
Voltage	6V
Headlamp size	–
Weights and capacities	
Fuel tank	2 (9l)
Oil tank	5½pt (3.1l)
Seat height	31½in (80cm)
Length	85in (215cm)
Wheelbase	56in (142cm)
Width	28in (71cm)
Ground clearance	7½in (19cm)
Weight	386lb (175kg)

in which the particular models were offered. As can be seen there were appreciably more different model/year combinations offered than for the A50, and the range also includes the Umberslade Hall framed 1971–72 models, which were never offered as 500cc models. Also the names used to describe the models seem to suffer from a degree of over complication and inconsistency during the 1963–65 model years. The 'Lightning Rocket' and 'Thunderbolt Rocket' models were renamed 'Lightning' and 'Thunderbolt' respectively after only one year. The 1965 'Spitfire Hornet' super sports model lasted for two years, before splitting into the Hornet (off-road) and Spitfire Mk II (road racer) in the 1966 model year. Which begs the question why was the 1966 Hornet not named the Hornet Mk II?

A65 Star: 1962–65

The first 650cc A65 road model was introduced in 1962 and was simply called the 650 Star, with the official model designation plain A65. The Star was also known as the Star Twin. The 'Star' designation was revised to 'Royal Star' for the

US and the UK in 1964, but confusingly did not appear as such in the factory brochures.

As with the A50 Star, the A65 Stars were the touring models of the range and remained virtually identical in appearance throughout the model's life. The engine was softly tuned, initially with a 7.25:1 compression ratio, which was raised early on in the model's life to 7.5:1. The introductory brochure for the range shows a star logo on the points cover – but no contemporary road tests or photos show models with this feature. In line with other makes and other BSA models of the time, and in stark contrast to today, there was no indication of the model's engine size or model name on the bike. The only way to distinguish between the A50 and A65 was by the colour or by looking at the engine number.

The headlamp nacelle housed the speedometer, ammeter, ignition and light switches, and a metal shroud covered the fork top yoke. The nacelle layout was poor, with the switches both located one behind the other on the left-hand side, and the ammeter was on the right-hand side. The ammeter was angled away from the rider and was difficult to read when in motion. A steering lock was conveniently mounted on the fork top yoke, with an access hole present on the pressed steel cover. The model was always equipped with the 18in wheels, shod with Dunlop tyres – a 3.50 section Universal on the rear and a 3.25 section ribbed on the front. Brakes comprised an 8in front brake in the full-width hub front and a 7in brake (rod or cable operated) in the semi QD rear. The rear brake was on the right-hand side of the bike, the opposite side to the brake pedal, so the crossover mechanism, with a shaft running through the swinging arm pivot, was used.

The bikes were dressed for touring with the heavily valanced mudguards and heavy-looking steel side panels, with winged BSA badges mounted on them. The chrome panelled petrol tank held 4gal (18l) of fuel, and was equipped with a reserve tap. These side panels were located at their front on rubber-mounted pegs on the inlet manifold, and by quick-release Dzus fasteners to the rear, and completely hid the single

---

Hunter S. Thompson

Hunter S. Thompson was the first of the 'Gonzo' journalists, who specialized in exploring the soft underbelly of American sub-culture. (Gonzo Journalism was a 1960s American phenomenon, which was based on the premise that journalism can be more truthful without strict observance of the traditional rules of factual reportage.) His peak was probably reached with his 'savage journey into the heart of the American dream' documented in his classic 1971 road and drugs book *Fear and Loathing in Las Vegas*. But his first real success was *Hell's Angels*, which was published in 1966. This book was a journal of his experiences with the Oakland Hell's Angels during 1964–65, when the Hells Angel phenomenon was starting to percolate through the American consciousness. In order to establish some form of credibility with the Angels he had to have a big bike. He chose a factory standard BSA A65 rather than the chopped outlaw Harley-Davidson that was the preferred ride of the Oakland Angels. Surprisingly, for a bike that was concentrating on motorcyclists, there is very little mention of the BSA throughout it!

BSA A65 Model Designations and Years

Model Code	Model Name	Frame Prefix	Engine Prefix	61–62	62–63	63–64	64–65	65–66	66–67	67–68	68–69	69–70	70–71	71–72
A65	Star (cable rear brake)	A50	A65	★										
A65	Star (rod rear brake)	A50A	A65	★										
A65	Star (rod or cable brake); note Royal Star in US	A50	A65		★									
A65	Star	A50	A65A			★	★							
A65	Police	A50	A65AP			★	★							
A65	Royal Star	A50	A65A			★								
A65R	Rocket (less rev counter)	A50	A65B			★	★							
A65R	Rocket (with rev counter)	A50	A65C			★	★							
A65T/R	Thunderbolt Rocket	A50	A65B			★								
A65L/R	Lightning Rocket	A50B	A65D			★								
A65L/R	Lightning	A50B	A65D				★							
A65SH	Spitfire Hornet	A50B	A65E			★	★							
A65LC	Lightning Clubman	A65B	A65D				★							
A65T	Thunderbolt	A50C	A65T					★						
A65L	Lightning	A50C	A65L					★						
A65H	Hornet	A50C	A65H					★						
A65S	Spitfire Mk II	A50C	A65S					★						
A65T	Thunderbolt	A65TA							★					
A65L	Lightning	A65LA							★					
A65H	Hornet	A65HA							★					
A65S	Spitfire Mk III	A65SA							★					
A65T	Thunderbolt	A65TB								★				
A65L	Lightning	A65LB								★				
A65FS	Firebird Scrambler	A65FB								★				
A65S	Spitfire Mk IV	A65SB								★				
A65T	Thunderbolt	A65T									★	★	★	★
A65L	Lightning	A65L									★	★	★	★
A65FS	Firebird Scrambler	A65F									★	★	★	
A70L	Lightning	A70L												★
T65T	Thunderbolt	T65T (1973–74 Only)												

Note that from 1964–67 model years the letter 'C' after engine designation (i.e. A65DC) indicated fitment of a close ratio gearbox.

In the 1967 model year brochure, BSA illustrated the cover with this shot of a Thunderbolt and Lightning. The lack of helmets and protective gear illustrates the carefree approach to motorcycling in the US market at that time.

carburettor. This was the ubiquitous Amal Monobloc of 1⅛in bore, which remained in this size throughout the model's life. A separate felt air cleaner was attached to the carburettor, rather than being accommodated in a separate air filter box mounted on the frame as on the A7/A10. As the carburettor was completely hidden, the remote tickler mechanism was fitted to enable a rider to flood the float chamber when starting. This comprised a pivoted bar, which pressed down on the standard tickler and protruded out of the front of the left-hand side panel.

Changes to the A65 Star and Royal Star models were evolutionary rather than revolutionary, and even the styling remained immune to the excesses exhibited by the more glamorous models in the range.

The model retained the nacelle and the heavily valanced, painted mudguards through to the end of the 650 Star/Royal Star models in 1965, when they was replaced for the 1966 model year by the Thunderbolt.

A65 Rocket: 1964–65

The first sporting model to appear in the UK and the US was the A65 Rocket (Thunderbolt Rocket in the US) in 1964. This model differed in both the state of tune and its looks from the Star models. The engine was tuned by increasing the compressing ratio (up to 9:1), fitting a sports high-lift camshaft, and using stronger valve springs and a larger carburettor – although still only a single instrument was employed. The carburettor was still a Monobloc, but had a 1⅛in bore. The clutch was uprated with heavy duty springs, which were longer and had a higher rate than those fitted to the Star.

Looks were improved enormously by BSA employing many of the classic British 'sporty' styling cues. These included losing the nacelle and its associated spring shrouds, having a separate chromed headlight mounted on chromed 'ear' brackets, rubber gaiters covering the external fork springs, a separate speedometer and (optional) rev counter mounted on individual brackets fixed to the fork stanchion top nuts on the fork yoke, a

The first A65 Star was identical to the A50 apart from the front brake. The bike was smoothly styled and clean in appearance.

siamesed exhaust system and slimmed-down 'blade type' chrome mudguards. The black-painted 7in diameter headlamp also carried the ammeter centrally where it could be seen easily by the rider while moving. It was flanked by the rotary light switch on the left and the ignition switch on the right. The steering lock remained on the yoke, but was easier to get to as the tin shroud used on the Star model had been deleted. When the optional rev counter was fitted, a revised inner timing casing and modified oil pump with drive were fitted. The side panels, however, were the same as those on the Star and continued to enclose the carburettor totally.

Paintwork for 1964 and 1965 was Flamboyant Red – a metallic bright red that would become the trademark colour for the Lightning when it replaced the Rocket. Wheels and brakes were the same as the A65 Star model with 18in rims, full-width hubs, with the 8in front brake. Tyres fitted were made by Dunlop, with a 3.50 section Gold Seal rear and 3.25 section, ribbed front. Performance was up over the 'cooking' model, with a top speed of around 105mph (170km/h) and the model was praised in the contemporary press for its mixture of low-speed docility and high-speed punch.

The model was used by the famous Isle of Man TT travelling marshals for the races held in June and September – a role that requires the best in performance, reliability, handling and road holding. However, it was only to last for two seasons, phased out at the end of the 1965 model year. The Rocket's sports mantle was taken over by the twin carburettor Lightning Rocket.

A65 Lightning: 1964–72

The 650cc Lightning model was introduced to the US market in the 1964 model year (as the A65L/R Lightning Rocket), and reached the UK market in the 1965 model year as the A65L. The Lightning was a progressive development of the Rocket with twin carburettors and revised running gear. It was even initially called the Lightning Rocket, with a model designation of A65L/R. The publicity for the model when it was introduced to the British market in the 1965 model year made great play of it being previously only available in the USA, and was described by BSA as having: '. . . super powered 650 twin-cylinder engine with two carburettors, special racing type camshaft, high compression pistons, unit construction four-speed gearbox, special "Gold Star" racing brakes. . .'

The main difference between the Lightning and the Rocket was the Lightning's twin carburettors and its wheels and brakes. The Lightning was fitted with twin 1⅛in Amal Monoblocs on a

new cylinder head that provided a 9.0:1 compression ratio. The model used 19in rims front and rear, the Gold Star type half-width 8in front brake and the BSA quickly detachable 'crinkle' hub at the rear. This brake was on the drive side, removing the need for the crossover shaft running through the swinging arm spindle, and required a new lug on the frame to take the foot brake pedal on the left-hand side. New slimmer mudguards were fitted, the front being the six-tab fitting type, with long tubular stays running from the bottom of the revised fork legs to the front and rear of the guard, and flat steel plates running up the leg to the middle of the guard.

The rear of the frame was also modified for the Lightning, with the rear sub-frame no longer forming a loop – known as the 'open' frame. The mudguard was bolted to the ends of each side tube under the end of the seat, and an additional support loop was run from the suspension top mounts to the mudguard below the combined rear light and number plate. The speedometer and tachometer were initially mounted on individual plates that bolted to the fork yoke top nuts as per the Rocket, but this mounting was

Model A65

The final year for the 650cc Star was 1966. Changes from the 1962 model were minimal, and in appearance the final model was virtually identical.

A65 Star Specifications			
	A65 Star (1963)	**A65 Star (1964)**	**A65 Star (1965)**
Engine			
Compression ratio	7.25:1 (mid 62 – 7.5:1)	7.5:1	7.5:1
Ignition	Coil	Coil	Coil
Bore & stroke	75 × 74mm	75 × 74mm	75 × 74mm
Carburettor			
Number			Single
Type (Amal)	Monobloc	Monobloc	Monobloc
Size	1⅛in	1⅛in	1⅛in
Transmission – sprockets			
Engine	28	28	28
Clutch	58	58	58
Gearbox (solo)	20	20	20
Gearbox (sidecar)	17	17	17
Rear wheel (solo)	42	42	42
Rear wheel (sidecar)	42	42	42
Gearing			
Top gear (solo)	4.35	4.35	4.56
Third gear (solo)	5.13	4.98	5.24
Second gear (solo)	7.18	6.96	7.32
First gear (solo)	11.1	10.92	11.51
Brakes			
Front (diameter)	8in	8in	8in
Front hub	Cast iron, full-width	Cast iron, full-width	Cast iron, full-width
Rear (diameter)	7in	7in	7in
Rear hub	Cast iron, full-width	Cast iron, full-width	Cast iron, full-width
Tyres			
Front (size)	3.25 × 18	3.25 × 18	3.25 × 18
Front (type)	Ribbed	Ribbed	Ribbed
Rear (size)	3.50 × 18	3.50 × 18	3.50 × 18
Rear (type)	Universal	Gold Seal	Gold Seal
Electrics			
Voltage	6V	6 (12V option)	6 (12V option)
Headlamp size	7in	7in	7in
Weights and capacities			
Fuel tank	4gal (18l)	4gal (18l)	4gal (18l)
Oil tank	6pt (3.3l)	5½pt (3.1l)	5½pt (3.1l)
Seat height	31½in (80cm)	30½in (77.5cm)	30½in (77.5cm)
Length	81in (206cm)	81in (206cm)	81in (206cm)
Wheelbase	54½in (138.5cm)	54½in (138.5cm)	54½in (138.5cm)
Width	28in (71cm)	28in (71cm)	28in (71cm)
Ground clearance	7in (17.8cm)	7in (17.8cm)	7in (17.8cm)
Weight	390lb (177kg)	390lb (177kg)	390lb (177kg)

The Rocket was introduced in 1964 as a sports variant. Separate headlamp and matched speedometer and rev-counter provided the sports appearance, and a lightly tuned single carb motor provided the go.

A brace of Unit Twins on the 2003 Fleet Lions run. The single carburettor Rocket in the foreground sports a later Lightning front brake and contrasts with the Star behind.

A65 Rocket Specifications

	A65 Rocket (1963–4)	A65 Rocket (1964–5)
Engine		
Compression ratio	9.0:1	9.0:1
Ignition	Coil	Coil
Bore & stroke	75 × 74mm	75 × 74mm
Carburettor		
Number	Single	Single
Type (Amal)	Monobloc	Monobloc
Size (in)	1⅛in	1⅛in
Transmission – sprockets		
Engine	28	28
Clutch	58	58
Gearbox (solo)	20	20
Gearbox (sidecar)	17	17
Rear wheel (solo)	42	42
Rear wheel (sidecar)	42	42
Gearing		
Top gear (solo)	4.56	4.56
Third gear (solo)	5.24	5.24
Second gear (solo)	7.32	7.32
First gear (solo)	11.51	11.51
Brakes		
Front (diameter)	8in	8in
Front hub	Cast iron, full-width	Cast iron, full-width
Rear (diameter)	7in	7in
Rear hub	Cast iron, full-width	Cast iron, full-width
Tyres		
Front (size)	3.25 × 18	3.25 × 18
Front (type)	Ribbed	Ribbed
Rear (size)	3.50 × 18	3.50 × 18
Rear (type)	Gold Seal	Gold Seal
Electrics		
Voltage	6 (12V option)	6 (12V option)
Headlamp size	7in	7in
Weights and capacities		
Fuel tank	4gal (18l)	4gal (18l)
Oil tank	5½pt (3.1l)	5½pt (3.1l)
Seat height	30½in (77.5cm)	30½in (77.5cm)
Length	81in (206cm)	81in (206cm)
Wheelbase	54½in (138.5cm)	54½in (138.5cm)
Width	28in (71cm)	28in (71cm)
Ground clearance	7in (17.8cm)	7in (17.8cm)
Weight	390lb (177kg)	390lb (177kg)

revised to the well-known alloy plate that bolted to the top yoke very early on. Six-volt electrics were fitted as standard, although the change over to 12V started during the 1965 model year. The instruments were magnetic type with grey faces.

Initially, the Lightning was available in Metallic Pale Gold with red pin striping on the fuel tank and the glass-fibre side panels. This colour echoed the sporting A10 'Golden Flash' model of the 1950s. The tank side panels were chromed, while the frame and fork legs were in black. Chromed mudguards, rear brake plate, headlamp supports and headlamp completed the looks, along with the corporate pear-shaped red 3D badges on the tank, and gold and black winged circle alloy BSA badges on the side panels.

A clubman's racer development of the Lightning existed for the 1965 model year and was called the Lightning Clubman. This was the existing Lightning model with rear mounted footrests, brake pedal and gear change, a single racing seat with a large rear hump (with a Gold Star-style round badge on the back), revised silencer and down-swept handlebars – also known by the coffee bar cowboys of the time as ace bars. The bike made for an effective 'out of the crate' café racer. In appearance, it was identical to the 500cc Cyclone Clubman.

The following year, 1966, saw the Lightning gaining a lower first gear and lower overall gearing, slightly larger inlet valves and twin silencers to provide more usable performance. Twelve-volt electrics, with zener diode charge regulation, was not standard on the model. The colour changed to Flamboyant Red, which became the Lightning's trademark colour – it retained the bright red colour through to the 1971 Umberslade models. Forks were changed to the flat yoke type, with longer stanchions, and the seat was changed to the humpback 'race-styled' type, with BSA in gold lettering across its rear. The headlamp was changed to a slimmer type, still chromed, but carrying just a centrally mounted rotary light switch. The ignition switch was moved down to the left-hand side of the headstock.

For 1967 the main change was to the carburettors, which were changed to the then new 32mm Amal Concentric type. The US-market alloy cast rear light was adopted across the whole

The Lightning took over the Rocket's sporting crown in 1965. The main difference was the twin carburettor head with cut-down side panels to clear the pill-box air cleaners.

This mid 60s Lightning is in 'Clubman's trim, with its clip-on handlebars, the BSA racing style seat and reverse cone meggas all contributing to the 60s Café Racer look. The headlamp brackets are 'Gold Star' style rather than the standard chromed 'ears', and look better for it!

This factory shot of the Lightning and Cyclone Clubman's model shows the handlebar layout using ace bars. The instruments are mounted on individual triangular brackets fixed to the fork stanchion top nuts.

For 1966 the Lightning gained the trademark humpbacked racing seat, which was to adorn the rest of the range over the following years.

By 1968 the US and UK Lightning were identical apart from the smaller fuel tank for the US. By now, the model had gained Concentric carburettors, twin leading shoe front brake, a grab rail and transfers on the side panels.

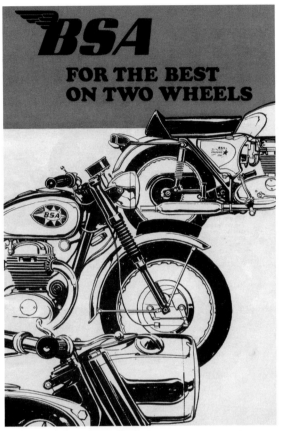

For 1968, BSA at last used the Lightning to represent the Unit Twin range. Strangely, the 175cc Bantam was in the foreground!

range. The engine gained the finned rocker cover, along with timing marks and a revised primary chaincase to allow for stroboscopic timing. The speedometer was changed to a 150mph (240km/h) model, and it and the tachometer were fitted into rubber pods, superseding the steel pods used to date.

The 1968 model year again saw evolution, rather than revolution. The major change was the fitting of the new corporate twin leading shoe (TLS) front brake, with new full-width hub wheel and fork bottoms to match. Suspension-wise, the fork gaiters were changed to be clipless, and the rear dampers gained exposed, chrome springs. New side panels were also specified, still in glass fibre but with flat faces, allowing a new crossed flags (US and UK) decal with 'Lightning' script. The US models gained a grab rail for the pillion passenger.

The headlamp sported a single oil warning light beside the ammeter and the rotary light switch was replaced by a toggle type. Engine-wise, the contact breaker points were changed to the Lucas 6CA type, allowing independent setting of the timing on each cylinder.

The 1969 model year saw little change in the bike's appearance, apart from the BSA logo being cast into the small circular contact breaker and rotor covers, and the revised TLS brake being

For 1970 the Lightning had gained a new tank, with chromed scallops for the rider's knees. The rear of the styling was unchanged.

A65 Lightning Specifications

	A65 Lightning (1964–5)	A65 Lightning (1965–6)	A65 Lightning (1966–7)	A65 Lightning (1967–8)	A65 Lightning (1968–9)
Engine					
Compression ratio	9.0:1	9.0:1	9.0:1	9.0:1	9.0:1
Ignition	Coil	Coil	Coil	Coil	Coil
Bore & stroke	75 × 74mm	75 × 74mm	75 × 74mm	75 × 74mm	75 × 74m
Carburettor					
Number	Twin	Twin	Twin	Twin	Twin
Type (Amal)	Monobloc	Monobloc	Monobloc	Concentric	Concentri
Size (in)	1⅛in	1 5⁄32in	1 5⁄32in	30mm	30mm
Transmission – sprockets					
Engine	28	28	28	28	28
Clutch	58	58	58	58	58
Gearbox (solo)	19	20	20	20	20
Gearbox (sidecar)	–	–	–	–	–
Rear wheel (solo)	42	47	47	47	47
Rear wheel (sidecar)	–	–	–	–	–
Gearing					
Top gear (solo)	4.56	4.87	4.87	4.87	4.87
Third gear (solo)	5.24	5.58	5.58	5.58	5.58
Second gear (solo)	6.75	7.8	7.8	7.8	7.8
First gear (solo)	9.29	12.27	12.27	12.27	12.27
Brakes					
Front (diameter)	8in	8in	8in	8in	8in TLS
Front hub	Half-width	Half-width	Half-width	Half-width	Full-width
Rear (diameter)	7in	7in	7in	7in	7in
Rear hub	Half-width, QD	Half-width, QD	Half-width, QD	Half-width, QD	Half-width,
Tyres					
Front (size)	3.25 × 19	3.25 × 19	3.25 × 19	3.25 × 19	3.25 × 19
Front (type)	Ribbed	Ribbed	Ribbed	K70	K70
Rear (size)	3.50 × 19	3.50 × 19	4.00 × 18	4.00 × 18	4.00 × 18
Rear (type)	Gold Seal	K70	K70	K70	K70
Electrics					
Voltage	6 (12V option)	12V	12V	12V	12V
Headlamp size	7in	7in	7in	7in	7in
Weights and capacities					
Fuel tank	4gal (18l)	4gal (18l)	3½gal (16l)	3½gal (16l)	4gal (18l)
Oil tank	5½pt (3.1l)	5½pt (3.1l)	5pt (3l)	5pt (3l)	5pt (3l)
Seat height	31in (79cm)	31½in (80cm)	31½in (80cm)	32in (81.3cm)	32in (81.3c
Length	85in (215cm)	85½in (216cm)	85½in (216cm)	85½in (216cm)	85½in (216c
Wheelbase	56in (142cm)	56in (142cm)	56in (142cm)	56in (142cm)	56in (142cm
Width	27in (68.6m)	28in (71cm)	28in (71cm)	28in (71cm)	28in (71cm)
Ground clearance	7½in (19cm)	8in (20cm)	8in (20cm)	8in (20cm)	7½in (19cm
Weight	398lb (180.5kg)	391lb (178kg)	391lb (178kg)	412lb (186kg)	420lb (192k

A65 Lightning (1969–70)	A65 Lightning (1970–71)
9.0:1	9.0:1
Coil	Coil
75 × 74mm	75 × 74mm
Twin	Twin
Concentric	Concentric
30mm	30mm
28	28
58	58
20	20
–	–
47	47
–	–
4.87	4.87
5.58	5.57
7.8	7.79
12.27	12.23
8in TLS	8in TLS
Full-width	Conical
7in	7in
Half-width, QD	Conical
3.25 × 19	3.25 × 19
K70	K70
4.00 × 18	4.00 × 18
K70	K70
12V	12V
7in	7in
3½gal (14.7l)	2½gal (11l) or 4gal (18l)
5pt (3l)	5pt (2.8l)
32in (81.3cm)	32in (81.3cm)
85½in (216cm)	87½in (222cm)
56in (142cm)	56in (142cm)
28in (71cm)	33in (84cm)
8½in (21.6cm)	7½in (19cm)
402lb (182kg)	383lb (174kg)

fitted, with the cable running down the fork leg to operate the new bell crank mechanism. This change also coincided with the use of Triumph type forks, which were double-damped using shuttle valves, with black headlamp shrouds and a revised front mudguard front stay, this being bolted to a fitting halfway up the fork leg rather than the bottom. The frame was also revised, raising the seat height by ½in and using phosphor bronze bushes in the swinging arm. Side panels were changed to steel pressings.

Engine-wise, much effort was spent on improvement, with the emphasis on keeping the oil in. This resulted in a 15 per cent increase in the width of the crankcase and primary chaincase joints, and an oil-pressure switch being fitted into the timing-side inner case. In addition, there was a partial change to Unified Fine (UNF) and Unified Coarse (UNC) American thread forms for many nuts, bolts and other fasteners. By the mid-1960s UNF and UNC were becoming the dominant standard throughout the automotive industry. As the US was the main market for BSA during the 1960s, the decision was taken to standardize on this rather than retain the traditional British thread forms.

The petrol tank was the major change in appearance for the 1970 model year when a new steel tank was introduced, with its styling based on the road-going unit single tanks introduced on the 250cc Starfire and 441cc Shooting Star in the 1966–67 model year. It was produced in steel with and a capacity of 3¼gal (14.8l). The Lightning model was painted in Polychromatic Red as usual, but both the indents for the rider's knees were finished in chrome. The year also saw the introduction of main beam and oil warning lights on the chromed headlamp. The engine improvements continued with a revised oil pump and modified cylinder block, using larger studs and with a strengthened bottom flange.

The 1971 model year produced the completely new set of oil-in-frame running gear (described in the following chapter). The Lightning retained its twin carburettors and speedometer and tachometer, and the major engine change was the adoption of a cast iron bodied oil pump.

A low-level exhaust system, with two megaphone-style silencers, was fitted. These silencers were prone to cracking around their mountings due to vibration.

Styling was completely different from the previous BSA look, the humped seat and chromed petrol tanks disappearing from the model for good. Probably one of the most striking and controversial aspects of the new frame was its colour. The frame was painted in an off-white colour called Dove Grey, which looked dirty before it had left the factory! The finish was supposed to look like a nickel- or chrome-plated scrambles frame, but failed abysmally. The side panels were a bit more restrained in plain bronze, and the 2½gal (11l) fuel tank was in bronze and white. Mudguards were chromed and front fork sliders were in unpolished alloy. Alloy brake and clutch levers were fitted to the new Lucas switch units, which controlled the standard indicators, as well as the horn, headlamp dip function, headlamp flasher and kill switch.

Few changes were made for 1972, the most significant being the adoption of a black frame and the larger 4½gal (20l) 'breadbin' tank, which was coloured in Metallic Firebird Red, as were the side panels.

A65 Spitfire: 1966–68

The Spitfire (A65S) models took the Lightning format of a fast, twin-carburettor road sports bike, and moved it up a level. Essentially, the Spitfire was a tuned Lightning. Based on the Spitfire Hornet Scrambler of 1965 (see below), the first true road Spitfire was introduced in 1966 as the Spitfire Mk II Special – the Spitfire Mk I (in the usual British traditions) never being formally applied, but being the Spitfire Hornet of the previous year (not the late 1950s A10-based Spitfire US model scrambles bike as some sources state). While the frame was the same 'open-ended' design as the Lightning, the

The first Spitfire Special – the Mark II of 1966 – had full road equipment, including lights, speedometer and tachometer. The fuel tank could be 2gal (9l) (illustrated) or 4gal (18l), carburettors were twin Amal GPs.

model was used to introduce one of the styling features that was to become a BSA trademark of the 1960s – the 'humped-back' seat, which was described as a racing pattern dual seat in the brochure. Full road equipment was fitted, including lights and speedometer and tachometer.

The Spitfire sported most of the seminal café racer's sporty gear of the time, comprising alloy rims, a restyled, glass-fibre 2gal (9l) tank for the US or 4gal (18l) UK petrol tank, and Gold Star full-width 190mm front brake. Surprisingly, although promoted as an out-and-out road burner, the model did not have the clip-on handlebars or rear-set footrests which had already been seen on the Lightning Clubman of 1965 as standard or as an option.

Wheels were 18in rear and 19in front, with 3.25 section Dunlop ribbed front tyre and Dunlop K70 4.00 section rear tyres – a Dunlop ribbed on the front and a 4.00 section K70 on the rear. The engine tuning followed the usual practice of raising the compression ration (up to 10.5:1) and

fitting Amal 10GP2 Grand Prix carburettors giving a power output of 54–55bhp at 6,900rpm. The camshaft was the same as that fitted to the rest of the range (with the exception of the Rocket) and the finish was Flamboyant Red for the tank and side panels, along with polished chrome-plated mudguards. BSA described the Spitfire Mk II Special of 1966 in its brochure as: 'It's the road racing version of the Hornet – it's the one with the built-in get up and go go GO!'

The performance was impressive, and fully justified BSA's description.

In *Motor Cycle*'s road test of April 1966 the Spitfire Mk II qualified as the fastest standard machine tested, with a fastest one-way top speed of 123mph (198km/h) and a mean of 119mph (192km/h). The Americans were also impressed, with *Motor Cycle* estimating the top speed to be around 125mph (200km/h) – although excessive vibration at the footrest and handlebars was mentioned. *Cycle World* (June 1966) was possibly a bit less keen, experiencing severe brake judder

For 1967, the Spitfire sported Amal Concentric carburettors. Alloy rims, 4gal (18l) UK tank and the 190mm Goldie front brake are in evidence.

A65 Spitfire Specifications

	A65 Spitfire Mk II Special (1966)	A65 Spitfire Mk III Special (1967)	A65 Spitfire Mk IV Special (1968)
Engine			
Compression ratio	10.5:1	10.0:1	9.0:1
Ignition	Coil	Coil	Coil
Bore & stroke	75 × 74mm	75 × 74mm	75 × 74mm
Carburettor			
Number	Twin	Twin	Twin
Type (Amal)	Grand Prix (GP)	Concentric	Concentric
Size	1$\frac{5}{32}$in	1$\frac{5}{32}$in	32mm
Transmission – sprockets			
Engine	28	28	28
Clutch	58	58	58
Gearbox (solo)	21	21	20
Rear wheel (solo)	47	47	47
Gearing			
Top gear (solo)	4.64	4.87	4.87
Third gear (solo)	5.32	5.58	5.58
Second gear (solo)	7.43	7.8	7.8
First gear (solo)	11.69	12.27	12.27
Brakes			
Front	190mm	190mm	8in TLS
Front hub	Full-width 'Gold Star'	Full-width 'Gold Star'	Full-width
Rear	7in	7in	7in
Rear hub	Half-width, QD	Half-width, QD	Half-width, QD
Tyres			
Front (size)	3.25 × 19	3.25 × 19	3.25 × 19
Front (type)	Ribbed	Ribbed	K70
Rear (size)	4.00 × 18	4.00 × 18	4.00 × 18
Rear (type)	K70	K70	K70
Electrics			
Voltage	12V	12V	12V
Headlamp size	7in	7in	7in
Weights and capacities			
Fuel tank	2gal (9l)	4gal (18l)	2gal (9l) or 4gal (18l)
Oil tank	5½pt (3.1l)	5pt (3l)	5pt (3l)
Seat height	31½in (80cm)	31½in (80cm)	32in (81.3cm)
Length	85½in (216cm)	85½in (216cm)	85½in (216cm)
Wheelbase	56in (142cm)	56in (142cm)	56in (142cm)
Width	28in (71cm)	28in (71cm)	28in (71cm)
Ground clearance	8in (20cm)	8in (20cm)	8in (20cm)
Weight	382lb (170kg)	384lb (170kg)	408lb (185kg)

above 45mph (72km/h), and criticizing the 2gal (9l) capacity of the petrol tank. The carburetion came in for especial criticism, with flat spots and rough running which indicated that the Amal GP carburettors would be a big headache to both riders and dealers. Surprisingly, bearing in mind the overall disapproving tone of the test, vibration levels were found to be low, in contrast to most of the other tests! *Cycle World's* test was titled 'Bomb from Birmingham'. I leave the reader to draw any conclusions from that!

The Spitfire Mk III arrived in the UK and US in 1967 with few changes in appearance from the Mk II.

When *Cycle World* tested the Spitfire Mk III in February 1967 it claimed that its test of the Spitfire Mk II had shown the machine to be below par, and that the development of the Mk III had been directly influenced by these comments – and there is some truth in this statement.

While the 1967 Mk III still sported alloy rims, a glass-fibre petrol tank (2gal (9l) in the US, with an attractive Red and Cream paint job, and the big, Royal Red 4gal (18l) job in the UK) and the 190mm brake, the compression ratio was dropped to 10:1 in the UK and 9:1 in the US, and, most significantly, the Amal GP carburettors were replaced with the new Amal Concentric range – although the main illustration in the 1967 US brochure still shows GP type carburettors, with a side picture trumpeting the fitting of Amal Concentrics! The UK brochure simply shows Concentric types. While the type of carburettor had changed, the choke size remained the same at 1⁵⁄₃₂in. The bike was well received by the testers, the brakes coming in for specific praise from *Cycle World*, being described as '. . . among the best of any touring machine we have ever ridden. The front unit, especially, is silky smooth and a marvel of efficiency . . .'.

This road test was a great contrast to the previous year's test, in which the juddering rendered the brake almost unusable! All Mk III's were fitted with the US-style polished alloy rear light unit with the Lucas type 672 lens (also irreverently known as the 'Tit' lens due to its similarity to that part of the female anatomy).

The final year for the Spitfire was 1968, with the Mk IV, broadly similar to the Mk III, but with the UK model's compression ratio down to 9:1.

As the years went on, the Spitfire was detuned and equipment was rationalized with the rest of the range. This US model has the 2gal (9l) tank, but sports the corporate TLS brake.

The main change was the adoption of the Triumph-designed 8in TLS front brake, giving much better braking and the use of end caps on the fork sliders to accommodate the Triumph type front wheel, rather than the push-through spindle wheel used for the 190mm Gold Star brake. While the tank and side panels were still in red, the colour was Cherokee Red. By now the performance advantage of the Spitfire over the Lightning had been eroded by the gradual detuning. The Mk IV was the last incarnation of the Spitfire, which was quietly dropped from the range for the 1969 season. The new 750cc BSA Rocket 3 three-cylinder machine was now the top of the range model, with a performance to match the new competition from the Norton Commando and Honda 750.

A65 Hornet: 1965–67

The first appearance of the 650cc Hornet (A65H) name was on the US-only Spitfire Hornet of 1965, a model tailored specifically for the US desert racing market which, to quote *Cycle World*,

provided: 'one of the few places in the civilized world with enough wide open spaces to permit full use of the Spitfire's shattering performance'.

The Spitfire Hornet was based on the 500cc Cyclone, and, apart from the obvious adoption of the A65 engine, the most significant change was the adoption of a longer swinging arm. This increased the Cyclone's 54in (137cm) wheelbase to 56in (142cm), and provided the Hornet with greater high-speed stability, which was needed due to the increased performance over the Cyclone. Wheels were 19in front and 18in rear, with 3.50 section front and 4.00 section rear tyres. The engine had twin 1⅛in Amal Monobloc carburettors and a 9.0:1 compression ratio. The underside of the engine was protected by a bash plate, mounted on the lower frame rails. Long high-level exhaust pipes with no silencers and a neat heat shield to protect the rider's legs ran along each side of the bike, terminating at the rear shock absorbers. No instruments or pillion footrests were fitted, although a flat dual seat was. Ignition was provided by a Lucas energy transfer system, which powered the ignition coils directly

The Hornet first appeared in the US as the Hornet Spitfire in 1965, and was renamed simply Hornet for 1966. An off-road model, it was the 650cc equivalent to the Cyclone and Wasp. This is the 1966 model.

from the alternator, and thus removed the need for the battery, which was omitted from the specification. High and wide handlebars, 2gal (9l) glassfibre petrol tank with alloy 'flip-top' racing style filler cap, chrome mudguards, knobbly tyres and no instruments finished off the ready to race appearance.

The Spitfire Hornet was renamed plain Hornet for the 1966 model year, and was still promoted as a scrambles model – again with no lights and an exhaust system the same as the previous year's, but with a much higher tuned engine to Spitfire specification, including a 10.5:1 compression ratio, although it continued to use 1⅛in Amal Monobloc carburettors. The sparks were still provided by an energy transfer ignition system, which meant that no battery was needed (or indeed supplied). As in the previous year's model, no speedometer was fitted, but a 10,000rpm tachometer was fitted on an alloy bracket attached to the top of the fork yoke.

While the model had the same gearing as the other 650s in the range, its off-road pretensions were addressed by fitting high handlebars, folding front footrests and a bash plate to protect the crankcases from contact with the ground. Again, no pillion footrests were fitted. Fuel was still carried in the glass-fibre 2gal (9l) racing tank, and the dual seat was now the hump-backed racing-styled version. While glass-fibre side panels were fitted, these were subtly different to those fitted to the road-going Lightning, although very similar in looks. As there was no lighting equipment, plain top fork shrouds with no 'ears' were fitted, along with a chrome rear mudguard that lacked any holes for fitting a rear light unit. Also for 1966 the West Coast US Hornet had a bigger oil tank, presumably fitted as a result of desert racing experience in the West of the US – the extra space was gained through deleting the tool carrier bag to the rear of the tank. The West Coast US model also had a single seat, presumably to go with the lack of pillion footrests.

For 1967 the Hornet retained its macho off-road looks, and gained Amal Concentric carburettors although this brochure picture still shows Monoblocs. High-level pipes and the small 2gal (9l) tank were fitted as standard.

A65 Hornet Specifications

	A65 Hornet (1965–6)	A65 Hornet (1966–7)
Engine		
Compression ratio	10.5:1	10.5:1
Ignition	Energy transfer	Energy transfer
Bore & stroke	75 × 74mm	75 × 74mm
Carburettor		
Number	Twin	Twin
Type (Amal)	Monobloc	Monobloc
Size	1⁵⁄₃₂in	1⁵⁄₃₂in
Transmission – sprockets		
Engine	28	28
Clutch	58	58
Gearbox (solo)	20	20
Rear wheel (solo)	47	47
Gearing		
Top gear (solo)	4.87	4.87
Third gear (solo)	5.58	5.58
Second gear (solo)	7.8	7.8
First gear (solo)	12.27	12.12
Brakes		
Front	8in	8in
Front hub	Half-width	Half-width
Rear	7in	7in
Rear hub	Half-width, QD	Half-width, QD
Tyres		
Front (size)	3.50 × 19	3.50 × 19
Front (type)	K70	K70
Rear (size)	4.00 × 18	4.00 × 18
Rear (type)	K70	K70
Electrics		
Voltage	6V	6V
Headlamp size	–	–
Weights and capacities		
Fuel tank	2gal (9l)	2gal (9l)
Oil tank	5½pt (3.1l)	5pt (3l)
Seat height	31½in (80cm)	31½in (80cm)
Length	85in (215cm)	85in (215cm)
Wheelbase	56in (142cm)	56in (142cm)
Width	28in (71cm)	28in (71cm)
Ground clearance	7½in (19cm)	8in (20cm)
Weight	386lb (175kg)	386lb (175kg)

The 1966 A65T Thunderbolt replaced the Star as the touring 650cc model. While it lost the nacelle, the mudguards were painted and the rear one valanced.

A US market Thunderbolt from 1967 has the optional tachometer fitted. The original caption read 'Twist the throttle for full-powered motocycling fun on a BSA.'

For 1967 the Hornet was toned down a bit, the primary change from the 1966 model being the adoption of Amal Concentric carburettors instead of the Amal Monoblocs part way through the model year (although in the 1967 US brochure the illustrations and the specification show the Monoblocs). The model was still aimed at the desert racer and still carried no lights or silencers. This was obviously becoming an issue, as the 1967 brochure carried the warning 'Machine must be fitted with lights and mufflers if ever used on the road'. The model was still competitive in competition, winning among other events the prestigious 1967 Peoria National in the US, but the writing was on the wall for the model.

A65 Thunderbolt: 1966–72

The A65 Thunderbolt was introduced in the UK for the 1966 season to supersede the A65 Star, at the same time as the A50 Royal Star replaced the A50 Star. The Thunderbolt then continued as the 'touring' 650cc model in both the UK and

US ranges through to the demise of the whole BSA range in 1972.

While taking over the touring mantle of the A65 Star it replaced, the Thunderbolt took its styling cues from the A65 Lightning model. The major changes from the Star were the slimming down of the general appearance, comprising the abandoning of the nacelle, the adoption of blade type front mudguards and the Lightning style of front fork with separate headlamp, gaiters and speedometer centrally mounted in a pod on the top of the fork yoke, giving a much more sporty look. The Lightning's open frame was also used on the Thunderbolt, and the Lightning's 8in half-width front brake was specified from the start. However, no tachometer was fitted. A single $1\frac{1}{16}$in Amal Monobloc carburettor was specified as per the Star model that the Thunderbolt superseded. While the Thunderbolt's engine compression ratio was, at 9.0:1, the same as the Lightning, the Thunderbolt was fitted with the standard cam, and its performance lagged behind that of the Lightning because of this and the single carburettor. The mudguards

By 1968 the US models were essentially single-carburettor versions of the Lightning but with no tachometer as standard. Chromed mudguards helped to lift the looks, but the Lightning's TLS front brake was not fitted.

This UK 1970 version was, like the Lightning, identical in appearance to the US version. By now the TLS front brake had been fitted.

Again, almost identical in appearance to the Lightning, the 1972 oil-in-frame Thunderbolt had also adopted the 4gal (18l) fuel tank and dropped the Dove Grey frame paint for Black enamel.

A65 Thunderbolt Specifications

	A65 Thunderbolt (1965–6)	A65 Thunderbolt (1966–7)	A65 Thunderbolt (1967–8)	A65 Thunderbolt (1968–9)
Engine				
Compression ratio	9.0:1	9.0:1	9.0:1	9.0:1
Ignition	Coil	Coil	Coil	Coil
Bore & stroke	75 × 74mm	75 × 74mm	75 × 74mm	75 × 74mm
Carburettor				
Number	Single	Single	Single	Single
Type (Amal)	Monobloc	Monobloc	Concentric	Concentric
Size	1⅛in	1⅛in	30mm	30mm
Transmission – sprockets				
Engine	28	28	28	28
Clutch	58	58	58	58
Gearbox (solo)	20	20	20	20
Rear wheel (solo)	47	47	47	47
Gearing				
Top gear (solo)	4.87	4.87	4.87	4.87
Third gear (solo)	5.58	5.58	5.58	5.58
Second gear (solo)	7.8	7.8	7.8	7.8
First gear (solo)	12.27	12.27	12.27	12.27
Brakes				
Front	8in	8in	8in	8in TLS
Front hub	Half-width	Half-width	Half-width	Full-width
Rear	7in	7in	7in	7in
Rear hub	Half-width, QD	Half-width, QD	Half-width, QD	Half-width, QD
Tyres				
Front (size)	3.25 × 19	3.25 × 19	3.25 × 19	3.25 × 19
Front (type)	Ribbed	Ribbed	K70	K70
Rear (size)	3.50 × 19	4.00 × 18	4.00 × 18	4.00 × 18
Rear (type)	K70	K70	K70	K70
Electrics				
Voltage	12V	12V	12V	12V
Headlamp size	7in	7in	7in	7in
Weights and capacities				
Fuel tank	4gal (18l)	3½gal (16l)	3½gal (16l)	4gal (18l)
Oil tank	5½pt (3.1l)	5pt (3l)	5pt (3l)	5pt (3l)
Seat height	31½in (80cm)	31½in (80cm)	32in (81.3cm)	32in (81.3cm)
Length	85½in (216cm)	85½in (216cm)	85½in (216cm)	85½in (216cm)
Wheelbase	56in (142cm)	56in (142cm)	56in (142cm)	56in (142cm)
Width	28in (71cm)	28in (71cm)	28in (71cm)	28in (71cm)
Ground clearance	8in (20cm)	8in (20cm)	8in (20cm)	7½in (19cm)
Weight	391lb (178kg)	391lb (178kg)	404lb (183kg)	413lb (187kg)

A65 Thunderbolt (1969–70)	A65 Thunderbolt (1970–71)
9.0:1	9.0:1
Coil	Coil
75 × 74mm	75 × 74mm
Single	Single
Concentric	Concentric
30mm	30mm
28	28
58	58
20	20
47	47
4.87	4.87
5.58	5.57
7.8	7.79
12.27	12.23
8in TLS	8in TLS
Full-width	Conical
7in	7in
Half-width, QD	Conical
3.25 × 19	3.25 × 19
K70	K70
4.00 × 18	4.00 × 18
K70	K70
12V	12V
7in	7in
4gal (18l)	2½gal (11l) or 4gal (18l)
5pt (3l)	5pt (2.8l)
32in (81.3cm)	32in (81.3cm)
85½in (216cm)	87½in (222cm)
56in (142cm)	56in (142cm)
28in (71cm)	33in (84cm)
8½in (21.6cm)	7½in (19cm)
406lb (184kg)	380lb (173kg)

The Firebird Scrambler, while still sporting high pipes, bash plate and folding footrests, has full road equipment fitted. Lights and silencers ensured that the bike was a definitive Street Scrambler.

A 1969/1970 Firebird Scrambler makes for an exciting ride even today. This example was snapped at the May 2003 Fleet Lions run.

were painted for 1966 and 1967 and then followed the Lightning in being chromed from 1968 through to 1970. While a blade type front guard, similar to that on the Lightning, was fitted, the rear guard was valanced.

The 1966 finish offered was the somewhat muted Flamboyant Blue as opposed to the Lightning's Flamboyant Red. In 1967 it was offered in Metallic Aircraft Blue, followed by Black for 1968 to 1970. The single Amal Monobloc originally fitted was replaced by the 28mm Amal Concentric instrument in the 1968 model year. The 1968 model year also saw the adoption of the Lightning's slimmer side panels, which left the new carburettor exposed. Running gear lagged behind the Lightning, with the Triumph type TLS front brake only being listed in the 1969 model year, one year after its adoption by the Lightning.

Thus the Thunderbird officially missed the first incarnation of this brake with its questionable long cable operation and only the later bell crank type was fitted.

The Thunderbolt was relaunched with the rest of the 650cc range for 1971, re-equipped with the Umberslade Hall oil-in-frame running gear. The model was still the tourer of the range with a low-level exhaust system, a single carburettor and no tachometer. The frame, like that of the Lightning, was coloured Dove Grey. The fuel tank was the small 2½gal (11l) item, and was coloured Stirling Moss Green on top, with white below. Side panels were in Stirling Moss Green. Mudguards were chrome.

Indicators were fitted for the first time as standard. A major retrograde step in the appearance of the Thunderbolt at this time was the offset speedometer, which was mounted on the right-hand side of the fork yolk. Without the tachometer to balance up the appearance, this gave an unbalanced look, which emphasized the economy model status of the bike. As with the Lightning, few changes were made for 1972, the main modifications being the adoption of the larger 4gal (18l) 'breadbin' petrol tank for the UK models; paintwork was Etruscan Bronze and the frames were painted black.

A65 Firebird Scrambler: 1968–71

The Firebird Scrambler (A65FS) was introduced as a US market model for the 1968 season as a replacement for the previous year's Hornet. The Firebird's main changes were dictated by its target market – while the Hornet was a pure off-road scrambler, the Firebird came fully equipped for the road with a speedometer and tachometer, a full set of lights and silencers.

The bike was not as highly tuned as the 1967 Hornet, but still had a 10:1 compression ratio and was fitted with twin 32mm Amal Concentric carburettors, which meant that the model was in a higher state of tune than that of the Lightning. The style of the Hornet's upswept exhaust system was kept, with one pipe sweeping back above the crankcases on both sides, but short street legal silencers were fitted, one on each side. The exhaust pipes kept the Hornet style heat shields, and in consideration for passengers heat shields were fitted on the silencers and pillion footrests came as standard, as did a large grab rail behind the dual seat. The Hornet's bash plate was retained.

The lights comprised the standard US specification alloy rear, while the headlamp was a small 6in diameter unit. The light switch and the dip switch were both carried in the unit, which did raise some comments in road tests as to the practicality of riding the bike at night. Lucas 6CA contact breakers were fitted, with the condensers fitted remotely. The energy transfer ignition system of the Hornet was dropped in favour of a standard battery-based system. The front brake was the TLS pattern in the Triumph full-width hub as fitted to the Spitfire and Lightning.

The front mudguard was the same as the Spitfire, with the front stay looping over the top of the guard and the ends bolting on to lugs on the centre of the fork legs, rather than using the six-lug design employed by the Thunderbolt and Lightning. All these changes indicated that the model was BSA's first attempt at a twin-powered street scrambler, rather along the lines of Triumph's on/off-road Trophy models. While West Coast US models had lowered gearing, the East Coast US model gearing was the same as the other 650cc models in the range. The glass-

ABOVE: The oil-in-frame Firebird kicked off with a Dove Grey frame in 1971, but by the time this early 1972 model was produced, a Black finish was standard.

The A70 looked identical to the 650cc Lightning. This bike sports a Rocket 3 Oil Cooler mounted under the fuel tank, a useful modification that both cools the oil and increases oil capacity.

A65 Firebird Scrambler Specifications

	A65 Firebird Scrambler (1967–8)	A65 Firebird Scrambler (1968–9)	A65 Firebird Scrambler (1969–70)	A65 Firebird Scrambler (1970–71)
Engine				
Compression ratio	10.0:1	9.0:1	9.0:1	9.0:1
Ignition	Coil	Coil	Coil	Coil
Bore & stroke	75 × 74mm	75 × 74mm	75 × 74mm	75 × 74mm
Carburettor				
Number	Twin	Twin	Twin	Twin
Type (Amal)	Concentric	Concentric	Concentric	Concentric
Size	30mm	30mm	30mm	30mm
Transmission – sprockets				
Engine	28	28	28	28
Clutch	58	58	58	58
Gearbox	E20/W17	18	20	18
Rear wheel	47	47	47	47
Gearing				
Top gear	E4.87/W5.72	4.87	5.41	5.41
Third gear	E5.58/W6.55	5.58	6.2	6.19
Second gear	E7.8/W9.16	7.8	8.67	8.65
First gear	E12.12/W14.37	12.27	13.6	13.58
Brakes				
Front	8in TLS	8in TLS	8in TLS	8in TLS
Front hub	Full-width	Full-width	Full-width	Conical
Rear	7in	7in	7in	7in
Rear hub	Half-width, QD	Half-width, QD	Half-width, QD	Conical
Tyres				
Front (size)	3.50 × 19	3.50 × 19	3.50 × 19	3.50 × 19
Front (type)	K70	K70	K70	K70
Rear (size)	4.00 × 18	4.00 × 18	4.00 × 18	4.00 × 18
Rear (type)	K70	K70	K70	K70
Electrics				
Voltage	12V	12V	12V	12V
Headlamp size	6in	6in	6in	6in
Weights and capacities				
Fuel tank	2¼gal (10l)	2½gal (11l)	2½gal (11l)	2½gal (11l)
Oil tank	5pt (3l)	5pt (3l)	5pt (3l)	5pt (2.8l)
Seat height	32in (81.3cm)	32 (81.3cm)	32in (81.3cm)	32in (81.3cm)
Length	85in (215cm)	85in (215cm)	85in (215cm)	87½in (222cm)
Wheelbase	56in (142cm)	56in (142cm)	56in (142cm)	56in (142cm)
Width	33½in (85cm)	33in (84cm)	33½in (85cm)	33in (84cm)
Ground Clearance	8in (20cm)	7½in (19cm)	8in (20.3cm)	7½in (19cm)
Weight	411lb (186kg)	421lb (191kg)	408lb (185kg)	395lb (179kg)

Note: Firebird Scrambler gear ratios are for US East Coast/West Coast.

fibre 2gal (9l) tank from the Hornet was retained, but was coloured in Red with white knee panels.

For 1969 the Firebird Scrambler saw a major visual change in that the exhaust system had both pipes swept up on the left-hand side of the machine, with twin silencers and a wire heat shield to protect the rider and pillion. The exhaust pipes were linked with an H-shaped pipe in front of the silencers, which reduced noise without reducing performance. The petrol tank was new, being produced in glass fibre and was of the sculptured pattern seen on the unit singles – although the overall style is that of a slimmed-down Spitfire tank. The front mudguard was changed to the Rocket 3 type with no front stay and a large central bridge piece, and the front brake operating mechanism was changed to the bell crank type. The engine benefited from the changes described in the section

on the Lightning. The dip switch was moved from the headlamp shell to the handlebars.

The 1970 model year again saw few visual changes. The tank, in Flamboyant Red or Blue, was produced in steel and had the knee grip areas highlighted in chrome. The compression ratio had come down to 9:1, and the rest of the specification, apart from the upswept pipes and the bash plate under the crankcases, was the same as that of the Lightning.

The Firebird Scrambler survived the changes to the range for 1971, and was produced with the in oil-in-frame running gear. As with the 1970 model, the bike was not a serious off-roader, but was in the US street scrambler mode, with the high-level pipes now in black chrome, bash plate and smaller 6in headlamp being the main differences between it and the Lightning. The 1971 model suffered from the Dove Grey frame, with an Etruscan Bronze and White 2½gal

---

The A65 in the Media

The BSA unit twin range has appeared over the years in film and in books. As a filmstar, the A50 and A65 can only be described as having walk-on parts, but they did appear in a number of notable films and TV productions both during and after their production run. The most prominent placing of a BSA motorcycle in the film world occurs in the 1965 James Bond film, *Thunderball*. The bike is a 1965 Lightning, in gold with a matching Gold Avon fairing. On each side of the fairing were two silver tubes, from which rockets were fired. The bike could actually fire real rockets, and did! The two rockets on a side were ignited using percussion caps from hand grenades, and were fired by the rider using additional air levers on the handlebars – one on each side. In the film the bike is ridden by the baddies, but is used to dispose of one of their own ('Count Lippe') in his convertible American car as Bond is tailing him in his Aston Martin. Once the deed was done, the bike is shown being pushed into a flooded quarry – although close inspection shows it to be an A10, the originals being saved to go on to assist in promoting the film. At least one of the bikes used survived, and has appeared in various classic bike magazines.

Bud Ekins, the famous Triumph and BSA dealer and stunt rider, rode an A65 in the car chase scene in the 1968 film *Bullitt* staring Steve McQueen. In the middle of the sequence, where Steve in his Mustang is chasing the bad guys, the action moves from the hilly streets of San Francisco into the surrounding countryside. As the cars race down a wide road, Bud on the A65 can be seen riding along, minding his own business and then having to take avoiding action as the two cars take up the entire road. The bike is laid down in the road, and slides past the cars on the dirt verge, with Bud sliding alongside.

The Lindsay Anderson film *If* of 1968 starred Malcolm McDowell, and was a classic teenage rebellion movie with a surreal twist where pupils at a school carry out an armed uprising against the establishment. The star rode a 1968 A65 Lightning, and is seen stealing it from a typical 1960s dealership during the film.

The Independent Television (ITV) series *Boon*, starring Michael Elphick, was a detective series based around a motorcycle courier company run by the main character. In the series, Elphick rode a late 1960s A65, and his sidekick 'Rocky' (played by Neil Morrissey) rode a Norton Commando.

The 2003 Jaguar advert for the X type diesel saloon features an early A65 Rocket or Lightning arriving at the petrol station as the Jaguar driver tries to convince the attendant that he does want to put diesel in his tank. It is, however, only a fleeting glimpse of the bike.

(11l) fuel tank. Side panels were also in Etruscan Bronze and the mudguards were chromed. The dip switch was situated in the handlebar switches and indicators were fitted as standard.

A70L Lightning and T65T Thunderbolt Models

Finally, the history of the range would be incomplete without mention of two further models, both produced in limited numbers during the last years of the BSA range.

The 1972 A70L Lightning was a 750cc version of the A65 and approximately 200 examples of this model were produced for the 1972 model year for the US market for use in flat-track racing. In the US they were also known as the 'Lightning 75', although this was not an official factory name. They used the Umberslade chassis and essentially looked exactly the same as the 'normal' 1972 A65 Lightning. They were not, however, just a 'bore it out' job – the increase in capacity was achieved by increasing the stroke, giving bore and stroke

of 75mm × 85mm. The compression ratio was also raised to 9.5:1. A large proportion of engine components were changed, and these included:

- crankcases
- crankshaft
- crankshaft sludge trap tube and plug
- connecting rods, including bolts and nuts
- big-end shells
- flywheel and bolts
- timing-side bush
- oil pump drive pinion washer
- crankshaft pinion
- crankshaft thrust washer to locate the crank positively against the timing-side main bush
- crankshaft shims
- oil-pressure release valve
- pistons and rings (available up to .040in oversize).

This list of changes indicates that an awful lot of work was put in to produce just 200 or so bikes – although looking at the modifications made especially regarding the positive location of the crank, it does beg the question of whether this

650 c.c. BSA T65

The T65 Thunderbolt was a thinly disguised Triumph Tiger 650. Note the use of the pre-71 TLS brake with the Umberslade-designed forks.

would have led to the modifications being introduced to the mainstream models. It is also interesting that the timing-side bush was retained, despite the experience that BSA gained in changing to a roller bearing during the Daytona races of the late 1960s.

This incredibly thorough approach to producing a 750cc model was the opposite to the approach Triumph adopted when increasing the capacity of the T120. Despite requests from the US, Meriden refused to develop a 750cc twin, so Triumph's American distributors took approximately 200 stock T120R 650cc Bonnevilles and slapped on specially commissioned big-bore barrels and pistons supplied by Rout to up the capacity to 750cc. These kits were fitted with the bikes still in their crates, and an extra 'T' was stamped on the crankcases after the T120R mark, making them T120RT. This 'T' was not stamped on the frame. The A70, in contrast, was an official factory model, and engine and frame were stamped up as such at the factory with the prefix A70L.

The final 'official' BSA model was the T65 Thunderbolt, which was produced in the 1973 model year to fulfil export orders for a number of bikes that stipulated that they had to be BSAs. By this time, production of all BSAs had finished, so the order was met by putting BSA badges on Triumph 650cc TR6 models. While these bikes used basically the same Umberslade-designed oil-in-frame running gear as the A65, they were the then current Triumph TR6, which by this point had had several modifications to lower the seat height.

Interestingly, these 'BSA' models were equipped with the pre oil-in-frame Triumph type 8in TLS front brake in a Triumph hub, rather than the conical hub and brake fitted to the 'normal' TR6. This modification necessitated modifications to the oil-in-frame Ceriani type forks. Approximately 264 were built at the very start of the 1973 model year during August 1972. Somewhat bizarrely, the BSA B50 was also made into the 1973 model year, but was badged as a Triumph, the T5MX, which reflected the state that the company was in during its last days

– having Triumphs badged as BSAs and BSAs badged as Triumphs!

Performance of the A50 and A65

The table overleaf take the published performance figures (top speed and 0–60mph times) from the contemporary motor cycle press. While much debate can be had regarding the accuracy of these figures, and whether the factory provided specially tuned (or well sorted) machines for the tests, the overall trends shown by the figures are interesting, and the figures do provide an indication of the relative performance of the various models.

Probably the most interesting comment to make is regarding the tuned Cyclone model and its touring stable mates. From these bare figures it can be seen that the Cyclone does have a significant performance boost over the touring models. However, in the test *Cycle World* commented that the gearing was far too high, being better suited to the Isle of Man TT races than US off-road competition. Better acceleration figures could therefore probably have been achieved, which would have brought the Cyclone's performance closer to the A65 figures if more appropriate gearing had been fitted.

These results show the significant performance boost that the extra 150cc gave the A65 over the A50. In addition, the results of tuning the bike to produce the Rocket, Lightning and Spitfire are illustrated by the significant performance increments each model displayed. The gradual detuning of the Spitfire is also shown, with the figures peaking with the Mk II, then declining slightly with the Mk III – while still maintaining an advantage over the Lightning.

Not surprisingly, the Thunderbolt demonstrated the performance penalty of its single carburettor with its consistently slower figures when compared to the Lightning. The biggest surprise is the 4sec 0–60 and 13.92 standing start quarter-mile figures recorded by *Cycle* for the 1971 oil-in-frame Lightning – on a par with a Spitfire Mk II and possibly indicative of a specially prepared engine.

Model	Source	Date	Top Speed (mph)	0–60 (secs)	Standing Start ¼ mile (secs)
A50 Star	*Motorcycle Mechanics*	Feb 1963	91	10	N/T
A50 Star	*Motor Cycle*	May 1964	96	N/T	16.6
A50 Star	*Motorcycle Mechanics*	Nov 1964	95	10	N/T
A50CC Cyclone	*Cycle World* (US)	Oct 1964	102	7.8	16.2
A50R Royal Star	*Motorcycle Mechanics*	June 1968	98	8.5	N/T

Note: Top speeds are average, N/T stands for Not Tested.

Model	Source	Date	Top Speed (mph)	0–60 (secs)	Standing Start ¼ mile (secs)
A65 Star	*Motor Cycle*	July 1963	98	N/T	15.7
A65 Royal Star (US)	*Cycle World* (US)	Feb 1963	106	7.3	15.3
A65R Rocket	*Motor Cycle*	Jan 1964	105	N/T	14.8
A65R Rocket	*Motorcycle Mechanics*	Apr 1964	106	8	N/T
A65L/R Lightning Rocket	*Cycle World* (US)	Jun 1964	109	6.7	14.8
A65L/R Lightning	*Motor Cycle*	Nov 1964	110	N/T	15
A65L/R Lightning	*Motorcycle Mechanics*	Apr 1965	112	6.5	N/T
A65SH Spitfire Hornet	*Cycle World* (US)	Nov 1965	102	5.9	14.3
A65L Lightning	*Motor Cycle*	Dec 1965	108	N/T	15.1
A65S Spitfire Mk II	*Motor Cycle*	Apr 1966	119	5.8	13.6
A65L Lightning	*Motorcycle Mechanics*	May 1966	108	7.0	N/T
A65S Spitfire Mk II	*Cycle World* (US)	June 1966	N/T	6.3	14.9
A65T Thunderbolt	*Motor Cycle*	Oct 1966	102	5.9	14.8
A65 Lightning	*Cycle* (US)	Mar 1967	104	6.91	14.5
A65S Spitfire Mk III	*Cycle World* (US)	Feb 1967	117	5.4	14.3
A65S Spitfire Mk III	*Motorcycle Mechanics*	Mar 1967	105	6.50	16.2
A65T Thunderbolt	*Motorcycle Mechanics*	June 1967	104	8.50	15.2
A65T Thunderbolt	*Cycle* (US)	Dec 1967	98	7.4	15.51
A65L Lightning	*Cycle World* (US)	Feb 1968	102	6.6	15.29
A65T Thunderbolt	*Cycle Guide* (US)	May 1969	107	7.9	N/T
A65L Lightning	*Cycle* (US)	May 1969	108	7.0	14.38
A65FS Firebird	*Cycle Guide* (US)	Dec 1969	115	5.1	N/T
A65L Lightning	*Cycle World* (US)	May 1970	100.86	6.5	15.10
A65L Lightning (OIF)	*Cycle* (US)	Sept 1971	N/T	4	13.92

Cycle World timed the 1967 Spitfire Special Mk III US model at 117mph. This puts it just 2mph slower than the previous year's Mk II.

BSA publicity shots ranged from the sublime to the ridiculous. Here a 1968 Thunderbolt hides behind a tree!

Summary

The A50 and A65 range started with a low-key introduction of just two models, both sharing the majority of their cycle parts and being styled conservatively and offering average performance. However, within two years of the launch (the 1963–64 model year), the range had increased to offer no fewer than eight 650cc and two 500cc models – in touring, road race and off-road styles. This meant smaller production runs of individual models and a consequential increase in management and works' time and effort to ensure that the correct parts reached the line at the correct time. The number of bikes in the 650cc range was reduced in the following year to seven, but the number of 500cc models was increased to four, albeit due to the introduction of two variants of the Cyclone. However, from the 1965–66 model year production was stabilized at four 650cc models – a tourer (Thunderbolt), road sports (Lightning) super sports (Spitfire) and off-roader (Hornet/ Firebird) and two 500cc models, in road (Royal Star) and off-road (Wasp) trims. The Wasp was dropped for the 1968–69 model year, and the A50 was finally discontinued with the introduction of the oil-in-frame models in the 1970–71 model year. With the 650cc range, the Spitfire

The 1972 Firebird Scrambler was a great looking bike. Keeping it looking good with that year's Dove Grey frame was another matter.

was dropped for the 1968–69 model year, leaving just three models. Finally, in the last year of production an additional model, the 750cc A70, was introduced, making four models in production for the 1971–72 model year.

Despite the totally different engine ranges produced by BSA and Triumph, as the 1960s progressed there was a gradual sharing of cycle components between the marques. This was most noticeable in the adoption of common front forks and the TLS brake in the late 1960s. The policy resulted in the best components, such as the TLS front brake being adopted by Triumph and BSA, with corresponding economies of scale and easing of the complement of spares held by dealers. The culmination of this policy was the Umberslade-designed frames and running gear of 1971, providing a common frame, running gear and electrics for both ranges of twins. However, the sense of this

major update has to be questioned, and indeed was by the public press and factory personnel at the time!

The running gear of the BSA and Triumphs of the time was generally acknowledged to be superior to that of their Japanese rivals, but the British engines, based on designs of the 1930s and 1940s, were much less sophisticated and reliable than the Japanese competitors. Possibly the only advantage the Japanese had at that time in their running gear was the introduction of disc brakes on the upper reaches of their ranges; BSA missed out on this trend by the introduction of a new drum front brake rather than a disc. Perhaps if the effort put into the redesign of frames and forks had been used to redesign the engines in the ranges, the course of the decline of the British motorcycle industry could have been halted.

3 Technical Description and Development

Introduction

The BSA A65 family of motorcycles was contemporary with, and in competition with, the Triumph unit 650 motorcycles, the T120 Bonneville and the TR6 Tiger. History has demonstrated that the Triumph won the hearts and minds of the motorcycling public due to a combination of success in competition and superb styling. However, this superiority of Triumph did not extend to the chassis, as demonstrated by the use of Triumph motors in specials such as Tritons and Tribsas. This indicates that the BSA all-welded frame was preferred to the earlier Triumph frames – however, how many Tribsas were made using A7 rather than A50 frames is a moot point!

The public perceived that the Triumph engine was easily tuned, reliable and quick, but that the chassis and running gear left a bit to be desired. There was a great deal of official and unofficial advice, guidance, expertise and tuning parts available to enhance the performance of Triumph motors, leading to a good deal of success in production and endurance racing, all achieved with only limited factory backing. In contrast, the A65 engine made little impact in competition. While it was successful in sidecar racing, apart from some notable exceptions solo racing success evaded it. There was no official long-term BSA solo racing sponsorship or programme, and few performance specials were built using BSA power plants. Despite this, it is an interesting fact that the later works Triumph Bonnevilles used BSA Spitfire cam profiles (E6897 inlet, E6988 exhaust) rather than the

Despite the championing of craftsmanship, BSA also recognized the role machines played in the production of their motorcycles. The 1965 brochure also had this picture, showing the machine used to 'shave' gears to remove 'stubble' – making the gears ready to give 'thousands of miles of smooth and silent running'.

Triumph-designed E3134 profiles so beloved of amateur Triumph tuners to this day.

Engine Layout and Design

The major difference of the engine layout of the A50 and A65 to that of the A7/A10 range is that the engine and gearbox were combined in a single unit. There were a number of advantages to this layout, including less weight, fewer parts and a rigid construction, leading to a cheaper motor to produce. It was also physically smaller, leading to a 2in reduction in wheelbase and eased maintenance for the rider – for example, primary chain adjustment no longer involved moving the gearbox. Last but not least, the unit construction resulted in a modern, clean appearance. Bore and stroke of the A50 was 65.5mm by 74mm, giving 499cc, while the A65 had an almost square bore and stroke of 75mm by 74mm, giving a capacity of 654cc, which could lead to discussions with insurance companies of the time, who had a 650cc limit on some policies.

The engine had a similar layout to the A7/A10; however, there were no common parts between the ranges, and the A50/A65 engine had been considerably 'beefed-up' in terms of the bearing sizes used. The engine's heart was a substantial one-piece crankshaft with bolted-on central flywheel, and plain, white metal timing-side main bearing and big ends.

A single gear-driven camshaft was positioned behind the crankshaft, and was driven at half engine speed by an intermediate gear driven by a pinion on the right-hand side (timing side) of the crankshaft. A timed breather valve sat at the left-hand side (drive side) end of the camshaft. Above the crankshaft pinion there was a scroll gear that drove a gear type oil pump. The ignition system was driven from the half-speed camshaft idler gear and comprised a mechanical advance/retard unit fixed by a taper, with the actual contact breakers being mounted on the outer case. The primary drive followed contemporary practice with the BSA four-spring clutch, but had a 'triplex' triple row primary chain. This drove the range's gearbox, which was mounted on a circular plate in the timing-side engine case, and was derived from the B40 unit single range, albeit substantially strengthened. This update to the pre-unit range was carried out at the same time that Triumph was doing the same with its 650 range, and the BSA and

The crankshaft was substantial, with a drive-side roller main bearing and timing-side bush. Oil feed to the big ends was through the timing-side bush, which could lead to problems.

The cylinder head was a compact design, with a large one-piece cover for the valve gear. Twin carburettors were introduced on the Lightning model in 1965.

Triumph Unit 650cc twins hit the streets in the same year, 1962. So there was immediate competition between the two, and it is worth revisiting this with the benefit of hindsight and analysing the strengths and weaknesses of the BSA engine through comparing it with the appropriate Triumph. The fact remains that the BSA A65 motor had a number of advantages over the Triumph unit 650 in design terms, and one disadvantage.

While the A50, with a bore and stroke of 65.5mm × 74mm was a relatively long stroke engine, the A65 had almost square cylinder dimensions (bore/stroke of 75mm × 74mm), which enabled it to have a much more efficient cylinder head/combustion chamber design when compared to the Triumph. The unit construction 650cc Triumph (the B-Series Twin) was, relative to the BSA, a long stroke design (bore/stroke of 71mm × 82mm), which theoretically resulted in less room for big valves in the cylinder head and hence less efficient breathing. Despite this apparent advantage, the valve sizes in the BSA were very similar to those in the relevant Triumph – a 1970 BSA Lightning had inlet and exhaust valve diameters of 1.60 and 1.41in, while the equivalent 1970 T120 Bonneville measured 1.59 and 1.44in.

An additional advantage that the BSA should have had over the Triumph was that, due to the longer stroke, Triumph piston speeds were higher than those in the BSA at given revs. This theoretically should have limited the revs that

the Triumph motor could achieve reliably in comparison to the BSA. This is reflected in the road test data of the time. Claimed power levels at the time reflect the BSA's superior head design – in 1971, contemporary US road tests have the BSA Lightning claiming 52bhp at 7,000rpm, and the 1971 Triumph T120R claiming 48bhp at 6,700rpm, both bikes having 9:1 compression ratios. Attempts to verify these figures from factory sources uncovered an interesting detail. The 1970 Triumph workshop manual give a power output of 47bhp, while the 1970 US Triumph owner's handbook says 50bhp (with straight-through exhaust pipes). All rather confusing, which is perhaps why BSA workshop manuals and handbooks of the time do not include any power figures.

In combination with the efficient head design, the BSA engineers took the layout of the A10 cylinder head one step further, and eliminated the need to carry the rocker shafts in separate rocker boxes – unlike the Triumph. The rocker shafts were carried directly in trunnions cast into the head, which proved to be an accurate and rigid assembly. The lack of separate rocker box or boxes also meant that all of the A50/A65 cylinder head bolts were bolted directly through the head into the barrel, making it easy to achieve accurate torque figures on these most vital of fasteners.

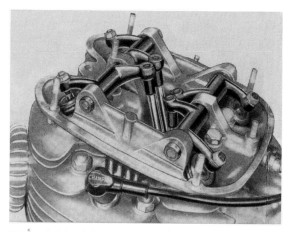

The one-piece tappet cover gave superb access to the valve gear. Rocker shafts were carried on pillars that were cast into the head, enabling the cover to be unstressed.

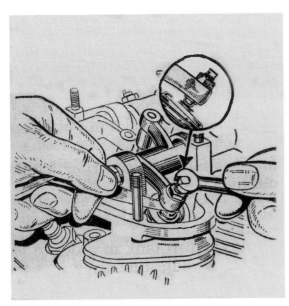

Tappet adjustment on the Unit Twins was an easy task due to the excellent access afforded by the design of the cylinder head. It was not so easy on a Triumph!

In contrast, on the Triumph Unit 650 engine, four out of nine head bolts were used to hold down the rocker boxes as well as the head, leading to a less than straightforward procedure to achieve a suitable torque figure for all head bolts. This feature was compounded by the compressibility of the paper or composite gaskets required between the rocker boxes and the head. This problem has only recently been partially solved with the introduction of solid copper rocker box gaskets for the Triumph twin engine. Two further advantages of the BSA system were that the rocker cover covered the whole top of the head and was unstressed, making it easy to achieve an oil-tight seal when it was on, and with the cover off you could see all four valves, rockers and adjusters.

At the launch, the rocker cover was smooth, helping to emphasize the overall smooth lines of the engine. On later models, the cover grew fins, making for an attractive and macho-looking top end, especially when sitting under the smaller US market petrol tanks – however, any extra cooling effect must have been marginal. The layout gave superb access to the tappets – no

fiddling about with small and loss-prone tappet covers as on the Triumph!

A final benefit of the head design was the easy refitting of pushrods to the rockers without the need for a special tool known as the comb, which was required for the A7/A10, or the fiddly task of blindly locating both ends of the Triumph pushrods before bolting down the rocker box.

Moving down from the cylinder head, the BSA top half had the pushrod tunnel cast into the barrels. In a stroke, this eliminated another problem area that Triumph owners are all too familiar with – stopping oil leaks from the individual inlet and exhaust pushrod tubes. The problems Triumph has with these are illustrated by the virtually yearly changes to these components and their assorted sealing mechanisms – changes that never really solve the problem.

Overall, the top end of the BSA was a much more elegant design than the 650 Triumph both in terms of production engineering, as it was easier to assemble at the factory and had fewer parts, and ease of use for the owner in terms of tappet adjustment and torque-down of the head bolts and nuts. It had fewer parts than the Triumph, was easier to assemble and dismantle, had fewer points that oil could leak from, and did not have anywhere near the same potential to loose tappet covers!

The bottom end of the BSA engine had some

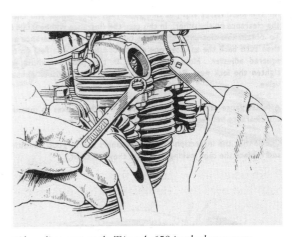

Valve adjustment on the Triumph 650 involved poor access.

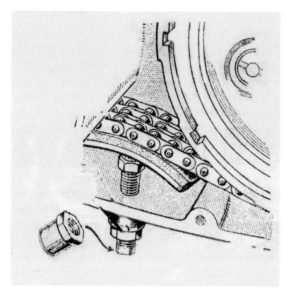

ABOVE: The primary chain tensioner was a slipper design. The rubber-faced slipper was adjusted by a bolt on the underside of the primary chaincase.

BELOW: Adjusting the Triumph's primary chain was a bit more involved!

advantages over the Triumph, and one major disadvantage. In the BSA engine, the layout of the single camshaft and the primary chain tensioner were both much better than those of the Triumph. The BSA has a single, gear-driven camshaft situated behind the barrels, as opposed to the Triumph's two gear-driven camshafts, front and rear of the barrels. The BSA system has fewer parts and less frictional losses – all in all an elegant design, using the minimum number of parts combined with good engineering practice. The application of these principles led to a system that needed virtually no maintenance.

The BSA primary chain tensioner was much more sensible than that fitted to the Triumph. The BSA had a silicon rubber-faced pivoted blade, controlled by a bolt screwed vertically into the bottom of the primary chaincase, while the Triumph had a sprung steel blade controlled by a long shaft joining the two ends of the blade together.

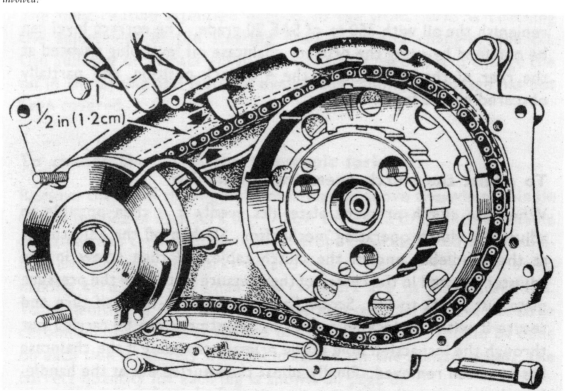

The BSA tensioner hinged on a rod that was rigidly supported at both ends, one in the left-hand side crankcase, and the other in the primary chaincase. The whole chain-adjusting operation was much easier and more straightforward than the Triumph's blade type tensioner. Accessibility to the BSA tensioner mechanism was easy, unlike the Triumph where the lower frame cradle obscured the adjuster hole. Adjustment could be carried out using a normal spanner and the operation was intuitive – screw in the tensioner to increase tension, out to decrease. The Triumph mechanism required a special tool – mainly because of the difficult access – and the feel of the mechanism was much more imprecise than the BSA, making it difficult to gauge if the tension of the chain was correct. In addition, the BSA mechanism was robust in comparison with the Triumph, which had the real potential for the tensioner blade to break if over-tightened.

The major disadvantage of the BSA engines bottom half was the perception that it had a weak bottom end. That there was a problem there is no doubt, but why there was a problem is more problematic. The bottom end had plain big end bearings, and two main bearings; the drive side was originally a ball race, (replaced with a lipped roller in 1966) and the timing side a plain bush. Oil was fed under pressure to the big ends through the timing-side bush. Filtration was minimal, with wire mesh filters in the sump and oil tank. As was standard practice at the time, a sludge trap was incorporated in the crank, which acted as a centrifugal filter to catch any solids before they reached the big ends.

This was the same layout as the A7/A10 engines, which had an excellent reputation for reliability, and there is no 'folklore' that says the bottom end of an A10 was suspect. In fact, many of the UK manufacturers' twins, early unit Triumph 500 and pre-unit 500 and 650s included, had the same layout, and car manufacturers had adopted this layout long before. The A50/A65 even had larger main and big-end bearings than the A7/A10. The A65's timing-side main bearing bush is 1½in in

diameter as opposed to the A10's 1⅜in, and the A65's big ends are 1¹¹⁄₁₆in in diameter as opposed to the A10's 1½ inch. When the engine was introduced to the press, great play was made about the strength of the motors and how the A10 design had been beefed-up.

However, while the early motors appeared to live up to this promise, as the design aged and power output was increased, problems started to appear. Power output was increased throughout the 1960s, going from a claimed 38bhp from the 1963 A65 Star to a claimed 55bhp from the 1966 Spitfire Mk II. This increase in power was achieved through progressive development of the engine. Camshaft forms and profiles were changed, which were complemented by increasing the inlet and exhaust valve sizes. The

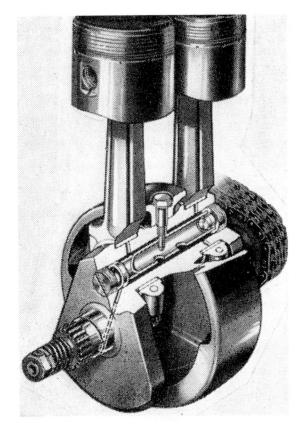

The crank incorporated a cylindrical sludge trap that fitted in the drilling connecting the two big-end journals. Debris was centrifuged into this trap before reaching the big ends.

carburettor size and the number of carburettors used were both increased from a single 1⅛in Amal Monobloc in the 1962 A65 Star to twin 1⁵⁄₃₂in Amal Grand Prix 10GP2 in the 1966 Mk II Spitfire. Finally, the compression ratio was increased, up from 7.5:1 in the 1963 Star to 10.5:1 in the 1966 Spitfire Mk II. While the bike's performance increased dramatically, the downside of this increase in power was increased stress on the engine, leading to increased wear on components. The problem was exacerbated with the introduction of the lipped roller main bearing on the drive side in 1966, which was more sensitive to the crank location and end float.

While Triumph and other manufacturers suffered from the same equation of ever-increasing power with little fundamental redesign work on the basic designs, on the A50 and A65 engines there was a critical design factor, which could lead to disaster. Once the plain timing-side bush had some wear in it, the oil pressure and oil volume fed to the big ends would progressively reduce, and as engine revolutions increased, oil pressure at the drive-side big end would be inadequate to handle the load, eventually leading to the drive-side big-end failure.

Another source of carnage was the effectiveness of the timing-side main bush location. Inadequate location of the bush in the crankcases leading to excessive end float on the crank could result in the bush turning in the cases. The oil feed to the timing-side bearing came through an oil way in the crankcases into a hole in the outer bush. The oil lubricated the bearing and then proceeded (against centripetal force) via a radius drilling in the crankshaft to the big ends. Turning of the bearing outer resulted in the oil supply being cut off to the main bearing – and the big ends – with catastrophic results. With the Triumph solution, the oil was fed to the big ends through the end of the crank, which proved to be pretty reliable even with worn main bearings.

A contributing factor to the motor's poor reputation may have been the introduction of multigrade and detergent carrying oils in the 1960s, which were sold as (and indeed were and still are) all-weather/all-temperature oils. This removed the need for owners to run straight 30-grade (thin oil) in the winter and straight 50-grade (thick oil) in the summer. Also, straight or monograde oils, in widespread use in the 1950s, would not carry impurities around the engine *ad infinitum* due to the lack of additives such as detergents. Small particles, such as carbon deposits, were either centrifuged out and deposited in the crankshaft sludge trap, or would sink to the bottom of the oil tank and sump, forming sludge, once the engine stopped. Larger lumps of solid matter (such as the white metal flakes from a disintegrating big end) would be caught in the wire mesh filters in the sump and oil tank. The use of monogrades meant that engines had to be treated to regular oil changes at least twice yearly in spring and autumn, changing the grade of oil as the seasons changed, which led to regular flushing of the internals. This need fitted in nicely with the recommendation from BSA for regular oil changes.

Conversely, multigrades were designed to allow for winter and summer use, and often incorporated detergents. The detergents were designed to wash combustion debris out of the engine and carry the small impurities around until they were filtered out using free-flow oil filters – very small particles would remain in suspension but were too small to do any harm to the engine. Black oil meant it was doing its job! This was common practice in the car world, which had long relied on plain bearings and had developed the full-flow filtration technology to protect them adequately – even before multigrades were in wide use.

BSA recommended the use of straight oil in 1966, but by 1969 was recommending multigrades, but with no relevant changes to the oil system (such as refining the filtration system) or amendments to the recommendations as to when the oil should be changed. The A65 oil-filtration system continued as before, little changed from the A7/A10 range.

This comprised relatively coarse wire gauze filters in the sump and oil-tank, which were arguably less than adequate even in the early

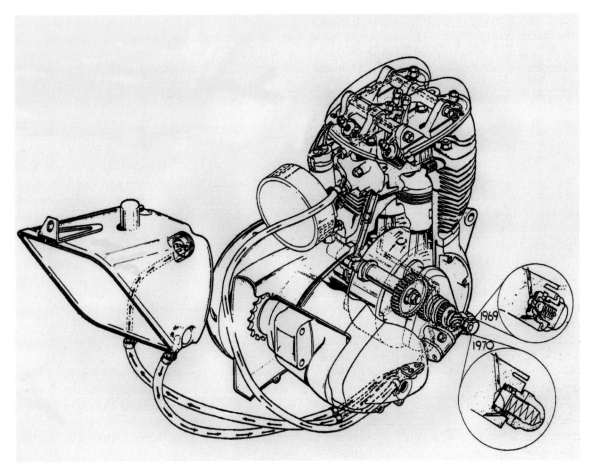

The Unit Twins' lubrication system was straightforward. The main problem was a lack of modern oil filtration, as only wire gauze filters were present in the sump and oil tank.

1960s, and a centrifugal sludge trap in the crankshaft. However, owners found that they did not need to change the oil as a necessity at the seasons' changes – in autumn the bike was no harder to start from cold than it was in the summer – so they did not. Hence, bikes were run with dirty and old oil, which compounded the problem – and a third or fourth owner running the bike on the cheap didn't help.

On top of these problems was the fact that the oil pump, a gear type driven from the crankshaft pinion, was alloy bodied and prone to distortion. This distortion led to a loss of oil pressure. Progressive modifications were made to strengthen the pump, culminating in the production of a cast iron bodied version in 1971, which had increased flow and a distortion-free body. It is generally considered to be fault-free, and a valuable 'retro-fit'.

Basically, it has to be said that the A65 unit could not cope with as much abuse as the Triumph twin engine could – the unit 650 Triumph bottom end had ball and roller mains, with oil fed directly to the plain big ends from the end of the crankshaft. If a Triumph was running its main bearings, it tended to give plenty of warning through noise and vibration, but the big-end oil supply tended not to be affected. In fact, in this state the Triumph engine was considered to give its best performance – the fact that

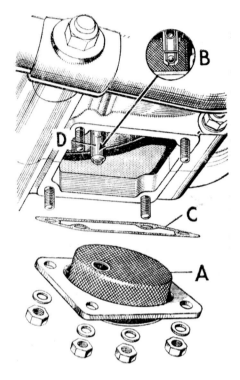

The gauze filter in the sump, while quite fine, was not as efficient as a modern full-flow filter.

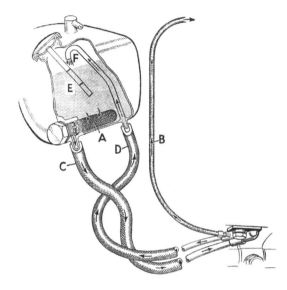

The same type of filter was present in the oil tank. Again, like the sump filter, it was not fine enough to stop all possible damage to the bearings from particles suspended in the oil.

Triumph engines usually ran best just before they blew up seemed to be the maxim of Triumph tuners of the late 1960s and is still recognized today. Looking at the Triumph's engine design this is probably correct!

Essentially, once an A50/65 timing-side bush was worn, then the engine was on notice of impending disaster. The first serious symptom would be a main bearing rumble and increased vibration, followed by a big-end knock. If ignored, these symptoms would result in a seized big end (usually the drive side) or a broken drive-side con rod – the severity of the damage tending to increase with the number of revs being used at the time. However, there are records of well-maintained A65s (that is, those having regular oil changes) lasting for comparable numbers of miles as the equivalent Triumph, although this does not take into account the differences between riders! I suspect

that in a controlled test, the Triumph engine would last longer than the BSA, as the bottom end is better able to resist wear and abuse without suffering a catastrophic failure.

While the BSA unit twin engine was gradually developed over the years, there were some significant changes towards the end of the life of the range. In 1969 the width of the crankcase, inner and outer timing cases and primary chain-case joints were increased to counter oil leaks, and there was a partial change to unified thread forms for many (but not all) components. Other developments to the engine included in 1970 the fitting of a revised barrel, with increased area to the base flange and larger studs (up from 5/16in to 3/8in) in modified crankcases. This was to combat some instances of the barrel lifting – usually in tuned motors. However, it was left up to outside firms such as Devimead to fix the fundamental problem of the timing-side bush, despite BSA fielding a team of racing A50s at Daytona in 1966–8 with just such a modification.

Carburation

The initial Star models were equipped with a single example of Amal's finest – the industry standard Monobloc in 1in size for the A50 Star and 1⅛in size for the A65.

This relatively benign carburettor specification reflected on the touring nature of the first A50 and A65 models. On the Star models, the carburettor was enclosed by the large side panel, which, while giving the smooth lines required, inhibited access to the 'tickler' that was used to flood the float bowl as a starting aid. To overcome this, BSA introduced a remote lever to enable the tickler to be used, which protruded out of the front of the left-hand side panel.

As the model was developed, larger and more sporting carburettors were fitted, culminating in the Spitfire Mk II for 1966, which was fitted with the ultimate British sporting carburettor, twin 1⁵⁄₃₂in Amal Grand Prix. These instruments were pure racing carburettors, with no provision for a pilot jet or throttle stop.

This meant that there was no way that a 'civilized' tickover could be achieved, as the only adjustment was through the throttle cable, which was connected directly to the throttle slide. Achieving a tickover was a hit and miss affair, totally dependent on the throttle cable adjustment, and hence the condition of the throttle cables – any stretch in which would directly influence the twin carburettors' synchronization throughout the range. With two instruments, as was the case of all unit twins fitted with GP carburettors, it meant that the chances of keep-

ing correct synchronization were virtually nil. This fitment resulted in so many warranty claims and complaints from the punters that the GP carburettor was dropped from the 1967 Spitfire Mk III, which had to make do with 32mm Amal Concentric carburettors, but suffered only a slight drop in performance as a result.

The Amal Monobloc continued to be used on the other models in the range, with two being fitted to the Lightning models and one to the Thunderbolt and Royal Stars, until in the 1967–68 model year it was replaced on all models by the less complex Concentric instrument.

The Concentric was so named because the float chamber was situated at the bottom of the instrument, with the main jet sitting in the chamber, surrounded by a ring-shaped float. While the Concentric offered little improvement in performance over the Monobloc, the chief advantage of the Concentric was its cost – it was substantially cheaper to produce than the Monobloc.

Unlike the Monobloc, the same casting could be used for left-handed or right-handed fitment, with the only differences being in the machining required for the tickler, pilot air screw and throttle stop screw. This instrument was used in both single and twin carburettor models until the range's demise in 1971.

On its introduction, the Lightning used a single cable from the twist grip, which was split into two using a junction box. This was a somewhat difficult system to synchronize as the

---

Devimead and SRM

Devimead was a successful BSA-oriented engineering company formed in the 1970s by Les Mason, who was formally employed in the BSA Competition department. Using his knowledge and skills he developed a timing-side main bearing conversion and end-feed crank to address the problematic main bearing problem – the solution was first seen on the 1966 Daytona A50s. The conversion comprised the replacement of the timing-side bush with a needle roller bearing, and converting the crank and inner timing cover to feed oil in through the end of the crank. This addressed the main weakness in the engine – the dependency of the oil pressure at the big ends on the condition of the bush. In addition to this, Devimead also developed other performance related modifications including a needle roller clutch thrust bearing, alloy clutch pressure plate and big bore kits. The company was eventually bought in 1986 by SRM, based in Wales, who still offer the conversions.

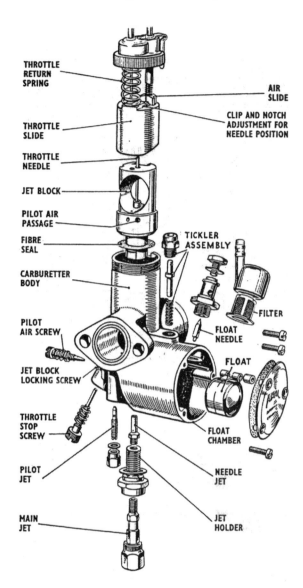

THROTTLE
RETURN
SPRING

THROTTLE
SLIDE

THROTTLE
NEEDLE

JET BLOCK

PILOT AIR
PASSAGE

FIBRE
SEAL

CARBURETTER
BODY

PILOT
AIR SCREW

JET BLOCK
LOCKING SCREW

THROTTLE
STOP
SCREW

PILOT
JET

MAIN
JET

AIR
SLIDE

CLIP AND NOTCH
ADJUSTMENT FOR
NEEDLE POSITION

TICKLER
ASSEMBLY

FILTER

FLOAT
NEEDLE

FLOAT

FLOAT
CHAMBER

NEEDLE
JET

JET
HOLDER

*The Amal Monobloc was virtually the standard carburettor
from the mid 1950s to the mid 1960s. While not ideally suited
to two strokes, it performed well on the majority of British four
strokes of the period.*

junction box was under the tank, so was replaced
quite quickly in 1966 with twin cables and a
suitably modified twist grip.

Air cleaners on the first Stars through to the
1970 model year bikes were, when fitted, simple
flat cylindrical 'pill box' types, which screwed
directly on to the carburettor. Initially, the body

of the single air cleaner fitted to the Star and
Rocket models was black.

As the side panels got smaller, and twin carburettor models appeared, chromed outers were
adopted across the range, giving a distinctive
appearance. It was all change in 1971, with
increased legislation over noise affecting induc-
tion roar as well as exhaust note.

The oil-in-frame models had an air box made
up of two alloy castings that wrapped around the
central large diameter oil-bearing seat tube. Two
gauze air-cleaner elements were mounted on the
outside of the air box, and filtered the air that
entered the chamber. The single or twin carburettors were connected to the air box by rubber
hoses.

In its time, the A65 probably had the widest
range of carburettors ever fitted to a single basic
model – from a single, unglamorous Amal
Monobloc through to the café racer's favourite, a
pair of Amal GPs. The range finished, like its
Triumph rivals at the time, with one or two
Amal Concentrics. It is interesting to note that
road models of the Triumph twins were never
supplied with the Grand Prix as standard – even
the sportiest unit 650 Triumph, the T120TT,
made do with twin Monoblocs or Concentrics.

Primary Drive and Gearbox

Drive was taken off the left-hand side of the
crank via a triplex ⅜in pitch chain to the clutch.
This carried five driving plates with friction
inserts and five plain driven plates, and had four
springs. The clutch drum was supported on
roller bearings. The gearbox on all models was a
four-speed, positive stop foot change mechanism
as per the industry standard of the time. The
design concept and layout of the gearbox was
similar to that of the C15 and B40 unit singles of
the range, but considerably strengthened. It
followed the traditional two-shaft British design,
with four pairs of gears on two shafts, the
mainshaft and the layshaft. Power was fed in
from the clutch on the end of the mainshaft, and
drive would be directed from there through the
layshaft, and then back out to the engine

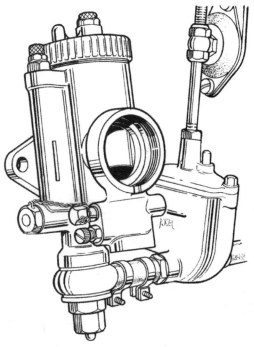

ABOVE: *The Amal GP carburettor was the ultimate 'go-faster goodie' for the 1960s café racer. It was fitted as standard to the Spitfire Special Mk II, but proved to be difficult to set up and maintain.*

LEFT: *As the carburettor was hidden behind the side panels on the early Star models, access to the tickler was facilitated by an extended lever that protruded forwards of the panel.*

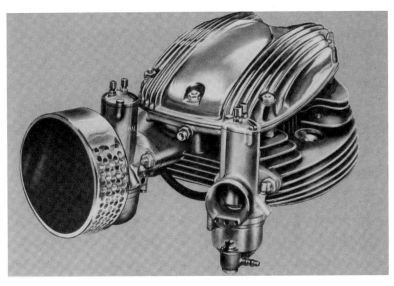

The Spitfire Mk III received the new Amal Concentric carburettor in 1967. Note the instruments are 'handed', giving easy access to the adjustors and the ticklers.

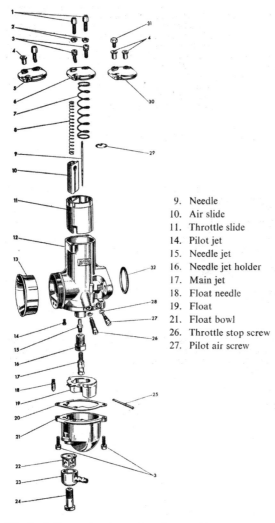

9. Needle
10. Air slide
11. Throttle slide
14. Pilot jet
15. Needle jet
16. Needle jet holder
17. Main jet
18. Float needle
19. Float
21. Float bowl
26. Throttle stop screw
27. Pilot air screw

The Amal Concentric took over from the Monobloc as the standard British carburettor. Its chief advantage was that it was cheaper to manufacture, and was available in 'handed' versions, making it more convenient to use on twin carb models.

sprocket which was concentric to the mainshaft and positioned behind the clutch. As usual with this layout, the clutch had to be dismantled to change the engine sprocket, and a circular cover was provided in the back of the primary chaincase for this operation. While the drive side of the main and lay shafts was located in bearings in the main casing as was standard practice in the industry at the time, the gearbox bearings for the

mainshaft and layshaft on the timing side were mounted on a circular plate that was bolted into a webbing in the main engine case, rather than being mounted on an outer gearbox casing.

This provided positive location of the shafts, reduced the stress on the inner timing cover, which only carried the kick-start mechanism, and probably helped to keep the oil in the gearbox where it belonged! Triumphs, in comparison, mounted the gearbox bearing in a separate inner gearbox cover, which was thus more prone to distortion and leaks.

A four-speed cluster was fitted through the model's life. The gear-change pedal was on the right-hand side through the life of the range, and the shift pattern was the Triumph standard down for first, up for second, third and fourth with neutral between first and second – commonly known as 'one down, three up', unlike the previous A7/A10 which was 'one up, three down'.

Apart from changes to ratios and hence the gear pinions, the overall design of the gearbox changed little throughout the production run – common part numbers being evident from the first and last versions for items such as selector forks. Note that the stamping of a 'C' after the engine number indicated that the factory fitted a set of close-ratio gearbox pinions to that engine – but there is no guarantee that they will still be there after thirty or forty years.

The primary chaincase has got provision for a final drive chain oiler built in. This relies on oil being thrown from the clutch basket on to the back of the chaincase, where it can then trickle through a hole provided in the rear chaincase fixing screw to a nozzle fixed to the back of the chaincase, and from there dripping on to the final drive chain.

Due to the provision of the full-width hub (almost) quickly detachable rear wheel, the speedometer drive was initially provided from the gearbox layshaft. This was changed to a separate rear-wheel-driven drive during the 1966 model year.

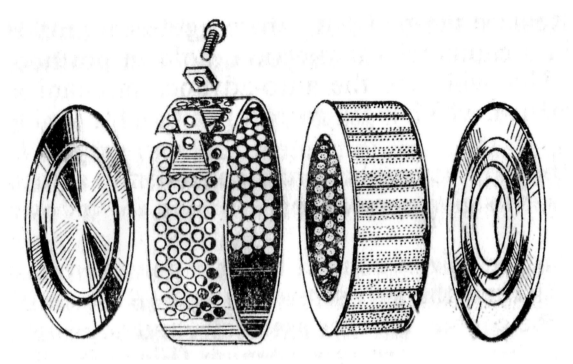

From their introduction through to the oil-in-frame models in 1971, when fitted, all models had 'pill box' type air filters, with removable elements.

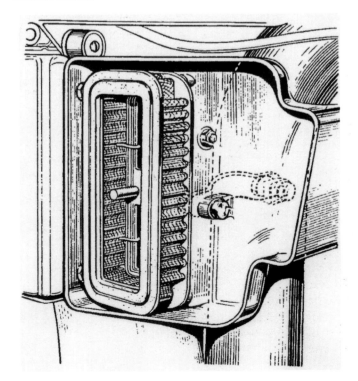

The 1971 models had a new air box, with washable gauze type filters incorporated. The air box was a large alloy casing that fitted around the central oil-bearing seat pillar of the frame.

Frame and Swinging Arm

The unit twins had two types of frame, the original 1962–70 model, followed by the 1971/72 Umberslade oil in frame. The original frame was all-welded, tubular steel, and was based heavily on the preceding A7/A10 range frame. This frame differed from what went before, in having a shortened wheelbase of 54in (137cm), giving an overall length of machine of 81in (206cm) and detail changes to the rear, where the oil tank was mounted between the frame loops, and the struts used to support the rear mudguard on the A7/A10 range had been deleted. The frame was a duplex design, so-called as it had twin downtubes sweeping down from the headstock that formed a cradle to support the engine before sweeping back up to join to the end of the main top tube.

The headstock was heavily braced, with the headstock tube being completely encased in sheet steel, which was wrapped around and welded to the downtubes and the two top tubes.

The top tubes comprised a large diameter tubular backbone going from the top of the headstock tube back to the nose of the seat. A smaller diameter bracing tube connected from the bottom of the headstock tube to the middle of this backbone. Two tubes swept down from

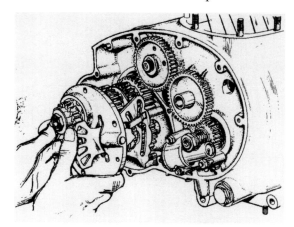

The gearbox is supported in the timing-side crankcase by a circular plate. Removal of the gearbox does not require the crankcases to be split.

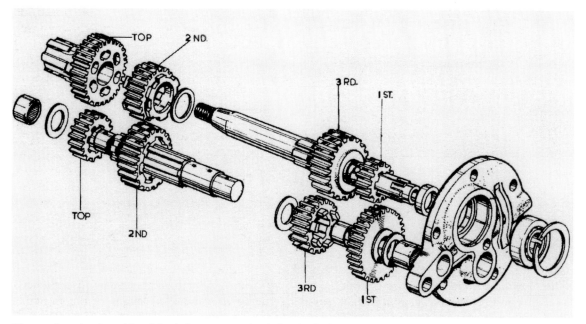

The gear cluster is substantial, and the shafts are supported on ball and roller bearings. The box has proved to be very reliable in service.

The rear chain oiler is fed from the rear of the primary chaincase. The nozzle directs the oil on to the chain.

the headstock, ran under the power unit and swept back up to meet with the end of the backbone tube at the nose of the seat. Plates to support the swinging arm were welded to the cradle, providing rigid support and location to this vital component. Ancillary brackets to support the oil tank and battery were also welded to this cradle. Seat height was quoted as 31½in (80cm). Two L-shaped tubes rising from the bottom of the cradle provided support and

positive location of the top of the suspension units. A further loop ran from the middle of these tubes back to the cradle to provide a mount for the passenger footrests. Steering head angle was 63 degrees.

The swinging arm was located on a spindle, with up and down movement being allowed by the standard BSA practice of two silentbloc bushes, which gave good if not perfect performance. The silentbloc bushes were changed to phosphor bronze in 1969, giving slightly better location and rigidity, and marginally improving the handling. The phosphor bronze bushes were also considerably easier to replace than the silentbloc bushes when the time came. The swinging arm spindle was located on a spindle, and fitted between the two flanges welded on to the cradle. It was held in position on the drive side by an oval plate that was welded to the spindle and bolted to the frame flange, and on the timing side by a nut and lock washer bearing against the frame flange. This system was simple, light and low maintenance, although the spindle could rust into the silentbloc bushes if not properly greased up. It provided 3in (76mm) of movement at the rear wheel, which was and still is quite acceptable.

The rear sub-frame, which provided the support for the seat and helped to locate the tops of the rear suspension units, initially comprised an oval-shaped hoop welded to the end of the backbone. The rear sub-frame was modified during the 1965–66 model year to be two individual stays running back from the shock absorber mounts, which were then bolted on to each side of the rear mudguard known as the 'open' frame, with the previous frame being known from then on as the 'closed' frame. This modification gave an easy recognition point between the early and the middle-aged machines in the range. This modification also coincided with the swinging arm being lengthened, resulting in the overall length of the machine increasing from 81in (206cm) to 85in (216cm). For the 1965 model year the modified frame was used by the Lightning and Cyclone models, and was adapted across the range for the 1966 model

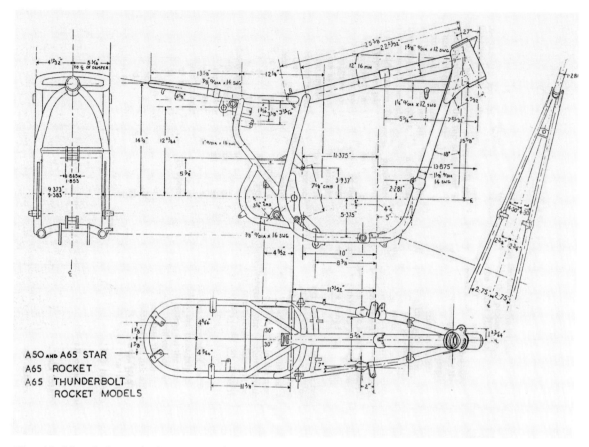

The original frame had a complete loop to support the seat. This type is known as the 'closed' frame.

year. In this modified frame, a separate steel loop, bolted to the shock-absorber top mounts, was used to provide further support to the rear mudguard and rear light. Minor changes to the frame in 1966 also led to the seat height rising to 32in (81cm). The frame was finished in black enamel from launch through to the 1971 model year, when the frame was superseded.

The whole frame was changed in 1971 with the advent of the Umberslade Hall-designed common frame for BSA and Triumph twins. At the same time, the A50 was dropped from the range, and was never produced with the new frame by the factory. The new frame was again an all-welded, duplex affair, with twin down-tubes, and its distinguishing feature was the oil being carried in a large diameter tube. This ran

from the headstock, under the fuel tank and then curved downwards to the base of the frame and was sealed off with a flat plate containing a sump plate, gauze filter and drain plug. According to popular opinion, the new frame led to a reduced oil capacity – but the factory literature states a capacity of 5 (British) pt (2.8l) – the same as the 1966 Lightning, although in reality the capacity is usually found to be over 4pt (2.3l) but under 5pt. However, the oil does run hot in these frames and an oil cooler is a sensible modification.

There is a possible explanation for this apparently retrograde step. Originally, it was planned to have the oil filler at the top of the big tube, just behind the headstock, but in production it was positioned under the nose of the

While the Unit Twins were not as popular with sidecar riders as the pre-unit A7 and A10 twins, they could be pressed into service. This 1965 Twin has a commercial box type sidecar attached, and appears to be being used for dispatch rider work.

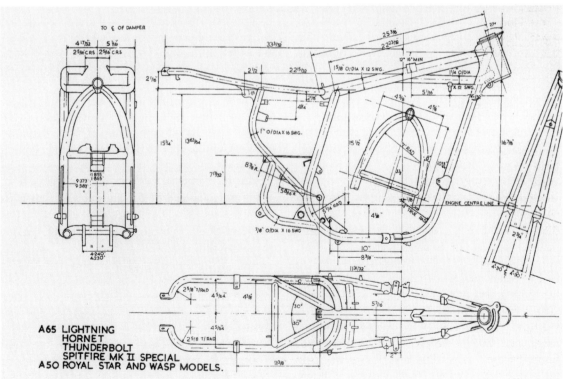

A65 LIGHTNING
HORNET
THUNDERBOLT
SPITFIRE MK II SPECIAL
A50 ROYAL STAR AND WASP MODELS.

From 1965 onwards, the 'open' frame slowly superseded the 'closed' frame. This frame had a gap in the rear of the sub-frame, and a separate loop was bolted onto the top of the shock absorber mounts to support the rear mudguard.

dual seat, in order to provide adequate space for frothing and expansion of the oil. This resulted in the oil capacity of the frame being reduced from a planned 6–7pt (3.4–4l) to around 4½–5pt (2.5–2.8l). It has been rumoured that the filler was not positioned behind the headstock because the factory was afraid that riders would mistake it for the petrol filler – but the positioning of the oil filler on the contemporary oil-in-frame unit singles in this position indicates that this was probably just a rumour! Twin down-tubes dropped from the headstock down to cradle the engine and then fix to the base of the oil-bearing tube. The swinging arm was supported on two solid bushes with good support to swinging arm ends provided by the engine plates.

The frame was considered to be a good handler with excellent road holding, and the design was used for the Meriden and Les Harris Triumph Bonneville and Tiger until the end of the production of these models in the late 1980s. The only drawback to the frame was the seat height, which at a reported height of about 33in (84cm) came in for some adverse comments from the press, punters and even from the factory engineers. Various stopgaps were used to reduce the height, including removing padding from the seat. A complete solution was found for the Triumph frames in 1972 by lowering the fixing points of the rear sub-frame upper loop, but it is unclear if this fix was ever applied to the last 1972 BSA models.

A final blow to the credibility of the BSA name was the colour of the frame on the 1971 models. While the Triumph Bonnevilles and Tigers had traditional Black frames, the BSA frame was painted in 'Dove Grey' – a sort of dirty off white. It was an unpopular choice by the factory, as it made the bike look dirty even when new. The rationale behind the colour was that it was supposed to look as if the frame was nickel plated, like some of the competition frames produced by firms such as Rickman – but unless it was a very dark, rainy night it certainly did not succeed! Customers were appalled, and the colour was changed to plain gloss Black

enamel for the 1972 models. Some dealers and owners were reduced to repainting the frame of 1971 models black, often not stripping down the bike to do this, resulting in an even worse appearance.

Front and Rear Suspension

The unit twins appeared with the BSA group forks, with the touring nacelle and shrouds. These forks had external springs and steel stanchions and legs. They were one-way damped and gave 5.75in (146mm) of travel and had a 63-degree steering head angle and 3.12in (79mm) of trail.

The forks were only damped on compression, and could and did top-out when under stress, resulting in some interesting clangs from the front ends of press-on riders! The top yoke was 'dropped', whereby the fork stanchions bolted into the yoke at a lower level than the top of the headstock. This meant that the stanchions were shorter than those used in later models, and that the distance between the top and bottom yokes, measured at the stanchions, was also shorter than the next incarnation of forks, introduced in 1966.

These forks had flat yokes, with slightly longer stanchions and different headlamp brackets to fit. These were also double damped, with damping on the rebound stroke, which made them much less prone to topping out, and gave a better ride. Travel increased to 6.75in (172mm). The head angle was changed to 61 degrees 12 minutes in 1970 with 4.47in (114mm) of trail, giving better high-speed steering at the cost of slightly less good low-speed handling.

The final models with the Umberslade-designed frame had a new 'Ceriani' type fork, with internal springs and alloy legs. The 1971 and 1972 alloy legs were supplied in a rough cast finish, with a thin polished rib running the length of the outside of the leg from the drain screw to the top. Later versions of the fork leg as fitted to Triumphs were in a smooth polished finish overall. No fork bushes were specified – the stanchions ran directly in the legs. While this

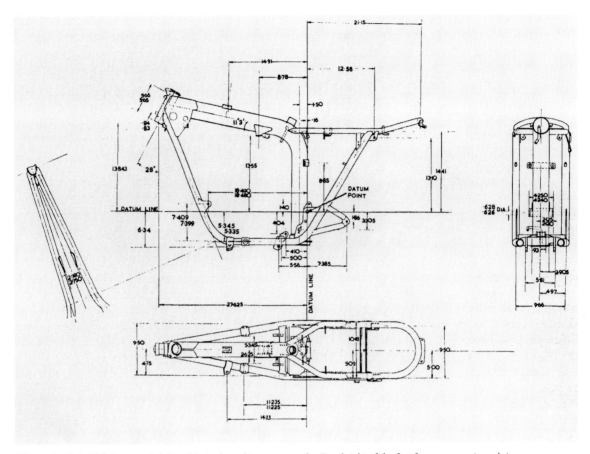

The Umberslade Hall frame carried the oil in its large diameter seat tube. Seat height of the first frames was an issue, being around 33in (84cm).

seems unwise, the forks do seem to last very well. The design featured exposed chromed stanchions with small rubber dust seals, and the steering head boasted tapered roller bearing, rather than the previous ball and cups. They were two-way damped, gave 6.74in (171mm) of travel and certainly looked up to date. Performance was considered good. A friction type steering damper was listed, but few bikes seem to have had one fitted. Handlebars were rubber mounted using Triumph-style bushes in the top yoke to support Triumph type P-shaped brackets. A steering lock was standard, and was mounted in the centre front of the top yoke.

One problem was found with the ease with which these forks could twist. By utilizing a four-stud fitting to secure each side of the front wheel axle to the bottom of the fork leg, Umberslade claimed that the fork was as stiff as those that had gone before and there was no need for a bracing strut at the top of the fork legs. Despite BSA's protestations, the fork was too flexible and the front wheel could be easily deflected from its path. The reason for this apparent design flaw may have been a styling and cost issue, as the front mudguard was supported on rubber-mounted wire stays, which looked good, carried on the theme of lightness given by the headlamp support wires and was no doubt cheap to produce. The later Triumph twins did have a bracing strut fitted.

On the original frame, the rear suspension was

The 1971 oil-in-frame bikes came complete with a Dove Grey coloured frame – which proved to be unpopular with the buying public. This is an A65 FS Firebird Scrambler, pictured in May 2003.

The early forks were fitted with 'dropped' top yokes, which meant that the stanchions were shorter on earlier models. The nacelle incorporated a top cover that hid all of the nuts and bolts.

provided by the silentbloc or phosphor bronze bushed swinging arm, with Girling shock absorbers, giving 3in (76mm) of movement. Initially, the springs and damper rods of the shock absorbers were fully enclosed, but as the 1960s marched on, the enclosures got smaller and the exposed rear springs were chrome plated, until in 1969 the enclosures vanished for good. This styling 'improvement' led to reduced life for the units as the damper rod was exposed to road dirt, which caused corrosion and damage to the oil seals. With the new 1971 Umberslade frame, the exposed spring Girling rear shocks were retained, but wheel travel was actually reduced to 2.5in (64mm) travel – a retrograde step.

Brakes

The brakes used on the first A65s, described as better than average in contemporary road tests, comprised an 8in diameter, full-width hub front and 7in rear. The A50 brakes were the poor relations, starting with 7in front and rear units, and only moving to 8in fronts for the A50C and A50CC in 1964, and across the whole range in 1965 – utilizing the same brake as fitted to the 650 Thunderbolt.

These first brakes were a single leading shoe (SLS) design, with relatively narrow shoes. Despite this, the 8in unit fitted to the A65 was well received, with the brakes as fitted to the Rocket described in a contemporary *Motorcycle Mechanic* road test as outstanding – giving them a score of 9/10.

Later forks sported flat top yokes, rubber gaiters and chrome headlamp brackets.

The A50 fared less well with its 7in unit, which was condemned in both road tests and readers' surveys as inadequate from its introduction. The A65 Lightning model of 1965 introduced the half-width 8in brake to the range, which had greatly increased braking area and slightly better performance than the 8in full-width unit.

A feature of this brake was the cooling holes incorporated in the hub – there were six small (¾in) holes as the brake left the factory, with six larger (1½in) holes blanked off, so an owner could knock out the blanks to provide even more cooling.

These brake diameters front and rear were to remain constant (with the exception of the 190mm brake fitted to Spitfire models) throughout the production run of the model, although the actual design of brakes used was changed a number of times. The width, and hence the braking area of the various front brakes also slowly increased in size. The

following table details the specific front brakes that were fitted to various models and gives the braking performance for these models as tested throughout the 1960s by *Motor Cycle* (MC) and *Motorcycle Mechanics* (MM) magazines in the UK.

Bearing in mind the rather subjective testing methods used to measure the braking performance, it appears that the optimum brake out of those tested is the half-width 8in SLS. The surprise is that the impressive sounding 190mm full-width Gold Star brake appears to be inferior to the 8in half-width hub. This was picked up by some of the contemporary road tests at the time; others just enthused about the use of the 'Gold Star' brake while ignoring its apparent inferiority. The major factor that the information presented here does not take into account is braking performance under stress – that is, how

The Umberslade Hall-designed forks were handsome and worked well. The lack of an adequate mudguard brace did make them flex more than they should.

The 1963 front brake was 8in in diameter on the 650cc Star but only 7in on the 500cc. In appearance they were the same.

The 1962 front brake was a single leading shoe type. The brake shoes were relatively narrow in comparison to the width of the hub at 1.12in.

ABOVE: The 1965 8in half-width front brake had greater braking area. Note the cooling fins positioned around the drum and the light alloy back plate.

The 8in half-width brake incorporated cooling holes in the back of the brake drum, further helping efficiency.

resistant each brake type is to fading through prolonged use. Perhaps there is a trade-off between one-off braking and heavy use, and the 190mm brake comes into its own in fade-provoking use. Certainly the relative braking areas of the two brakes, combined with BSA's undoubted racing experience with the brake on the Gold Star, imply that this should be the case. The 190mm brake with its 2in wide shoes has a swept area of 47.1sq in, while the 8in brake with its 1.62in width shoes has a swept area of only 40.7sq in. So on paper the 190mm brake should be far superior to the 8in, but this advantage is not shown in ordinary road use. Measuring the distance to stop from 100mph may show a different story, and this premise is borne out by the test of a UK model Spitfire Mk II by *Motor Cycle* in April 1966. The test stated in a picture

caption that: 'The race-bred 190mm front brake with full-width linings. It is very effective in killing high speeds.' and, in the text, said: 'Originally developed for racing, the 190mm front brake was in its element during repeated fierce usage from very high speeds. Power and sensitivity were sufficient to squeal the front tyre, though braking power at town speeds was only average.' So it does appear that for high-speed use the 190mm brake is superior to the 8in half-width brake, while the opposite is true for slower day to day usage.

Information on braking distances of A65s fitted with the 1968–70 Triumph TLS brake is scarce, but *Motorcycle Mechanics* tested the T120 Bonneville, getting 28ft 6in in 1968 (with the original straight cable operation) and 29ft 6in in 1969 with the revised bell crank arrangement. As

Model	Test Date	Test Source	Front Brake Type & diameter	Brake Width	Test Result – braking distance from 30mph
A65 Star	Jul 1963	MC	Full-width hub, SLS – 8in	1.12	29ft 6in
A50 Star	Feb 1963	MM	Full-width hub, SLS – 7in	1.12	36ft
A65 Rocket	Jan 1964	MC	Full-width hub, SLS – 8in	1.12	34ft
A50 Star	May 1964	MC	Full-width hub, SLS – 7in	1.12	32ft
A65 Rocket	Apr 1964	MM	Full-width hub, SLS – 8in	1.12	28ft
A50 Star	Nov 1964	MM	Full-width hub, SLS – 7in	1.12	37ft
A65L Lightning	Nov 1964	MC	Half-width hub, SLS, Gold Star type – 8in	1.62	27ft
A65L Lightning	April 1965	MM	Half-width hub, SLS, Gold Star type – 8in	1.62	26ft
A65L Lightning	Dec 1965	MC	Half-width hub, SLS, Gold Star type – 8in	1.62	33ft (damp tarmac)
A65S Spitfire Mk II	Apr 1966	MC	Full-width alloy hub, SLS, Gold Star Type, 190mm (7½in)	2.0	31ft 6in
A65L Lightning	May 1966	MM	Half-width hub, SLS, Gold Star type – 8in	1.62	30
A65T Thunderbolt	Oct 1966	MC	Half-width hub, SLS, Gold Star type – 8in	1.62	32
A65S Spitfire Mk III	Mar 1967	MM	Full-width alloy hub, SLS, Gold Star Type, 190mm (7½in)	2.0	34
A65T Thunderbolt	Jun 1967	MM	Half-width hub, SLS, Gold Star type – 8in	1.62	28
A50 Royal Star	Jun 1968	MM	Half-width hub, SLS, Gold Star type – 8in	1.62	32ft 6in

This 1968 US Market Thunderbolt is posed with an example of pre-World War II technology – the de Havilland Tiger Moth.
Note the small fuel tank, and the single leading shoe 8in front brake – the last year of fitment before the model gained the corporate twin
leading-shoe brake.

the Triumph and BSA weigh about the same, it is reasonable to assume that comparable performance should be expected from the A65 equipped with the same brake – again performance comparable to the half-width hub, 8in brake.

So the range started with the BSA standard brakes in 1962, encased in cast iron full-width hubs. The sporting models, starting with the Lightning, gained the half-width 8in cast iron front and 7in half-width rears in 1965, followed by the Spitfire with its full-width 190mm front in 1966. The cooking 500cc Royal Star tended to be a year behind the 650cc Thunderbolt in brake specification.

The Triumph 8in twin leading shoe front

brake was fitted to the Lightning and Spitfire Mk 111 in 1968 and to the rest of the range in 1969 (including the A50), mirroring the use of the brake on the Triumph range – although some of Triumph's less sporting 500cc twins had a 7in version, as indeed did the unit singles range in 1969. This 8in diameter, full-width hub brake used a system of rods and levers to translate the cable pull to both brake cams. The swept area of the brake was the same as the previous half-width 8in drum at 40.7sq in. In the first design of the brake, the cable was directed to the rear of the drum, and pulled horizontally. This meant using a long cable, and in use a number of design faults became apparent. Firstly, there was the possibility of the cable jumping out of the abutment on the

The 190mm front brake was only fitted to the Spitfire Mk II and Mk III. It provided excellent high-speed braking performance.

the brake. This brake was generally considered to be the best standard production front brake produced by the British motorcycle industry. It was robust, adequately ventilated to avoid fade, looked good and worked well. The only downside was that it could be tricky to set up initially and when changing brake shoes to ensure both shoes made contact with the drum at the same time. However, once set up, it was fuss-free, smooth and powerful. The famous Triumph tuner Stan Sheldon described the brake as: 'one of the most effective and reasonably priced standard production units on the market'.

Sheldon does, however, point out that it was nowhere near as good as the Seeley double-sided 8in unit, which came complete with its own magnesium hub. This was listed by Triumph as an optional extra, making it available for production racing, but how many were supplied for 'production' Triumphs is a moot point.

Initially, the rear brake was a 7in on both models, and was placed on the right-hand side of the semi-QD full-width hub. The brake was operated either by a rod or a cable, but in both cases the operating mechanism comprised a shaft running through the swinging arm pivot, with the brake pedal splined on to the left-hand end, and an actuating arm splined on the right-hand side. In 1966 this rear wheel was changed across the range to the famous BSA 'crinkle hub'

brake plate when some wear had set in. Drilling the abutment to take a split pin solved this, and the change was instigated quickly in the 1968 model year with instructions given to dealers to modify existing brakes. The second problem was the length of the cable. Firstly, its length lead to a spongy feel, and secondly it was routed so that it could get caught under the rear of the front mudguard when the fork was fully compressed, causing the brake to lock on with possibly disastrous consequences.

To solve these problems, the 1969 brake featured a redesigned operating mechanism, with the cable running down the fork leg, linking to a cranked operating lever. This also shortened the length of the cable, which improved the feel of

The 1968 twin leading shoe front brake was a Triumph design. The long sweep of the cable entering at the back of the brake plate could catch on the mudguard.

For 1968 BSA had a nautical theme for its publicity photos in the USA. This neatly posed Lightning shows the 1968-only twin leading shoe front brake, and the small US specification fuel tank.

The faults with the 1968 TLS brake resulted in a new actuating mechanism being specified for 1969, resulting in the 'bell crank' design.

Umberslade-designed frame. The new brakes were enclosed in handsome conical alloy hubs, similar in appearance (if not in performance) to the Norton Manx units of the late 1950s. The rear was an adequate 7in in diameter, rod-operated on the left-hand side of the bike as before, and seems to have aroused little enthusiasm or enmity during its life. The front was an 8in, TLS unit, described as fade-free in the contemporary literature, but generally referred to as comical when tested to its limit!

There is no doubt that the brake was not as good as the Triumph TLS that preceded it, but

The original rear brake was on the timing side of the bike. This meant it had to be operated by a crossover shaft from the brake pedal.

design QD wheel, previously fitted to the Lightning, Hornet and Wasp models in the unit twin range only.

This still had a 7in brake, but it was rod-operated and had a combined sprocket and brake drum on the drive side. The brake pedal was changed to one that pivoted on a separate lug on the frame, rather than on the rod running all the way through the swinging arm spindle. This brake then remained unchanged through to the 1971 model year, although the back plate material changed from steel to alloy for the 1968 model year. Up to the 1971 change of running gear, the rear brake operated the brake light switch through a neat rotary action switch that was positioned above the brake pedal. This switch was sprung-loaded, and when the arm fixed to the pedal was moved, it would turn on the brake light. This was an elegant design, and was much better than the usual pull switches offered by BSA's competitors.

As described above, the brakes and running gear of the A65 were changed completely in the 1971 model year, with the introduction of the

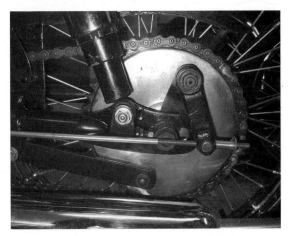

The post 1965 rear brake was in the QD 'crinkle' hub. It was rod operated directly from the brake pedal.

The rear brake light up to 1970 was operated by a neat rotary action switch. This was tucked out of the way of road dirt above the brake pedal.

The 1971 front brake was an 8in TLS unit housed in a conical hub. This illustration is of a 1972 model, with a black-painted back plate.

there is also a degree of folklore and legend that dictates that the brake was worse than it really was. There is no doubt that the same brake on the Rocket 3 was out of its depth – conversely, using it on the B25SS 'Gold Star' 250cc single was probably overkill! Generally, it seemed that the brake would work if correctly set up, but could not dissipate heat efficiently enough to avoid fade in heavy, prolonged use. Interestingly, the swept area of this brake was only 37.7sq in, approximately 10 per cent less than the previous Triumph type TLS brake.

The design of the brake was good in parts – the cable outer was mounted on one brake arm, and the end of the cable was fixed on the second arm. The theory was that this would provide equal, self-adjusting pressure on both leading shoes, resulting in a brake that was, in effect, always providing the same amount of braking

from both shoes. Interestingly, BMW used an identical method of operating its TLS brake on the R69S in the 1950s and 1960s. Individual adjustment of the two-brake shoe pivots was provided for using a standard automotive 'click-stop' mechanism, enabling easy and precise setting up of the brake. The brake design overcame the problem of balancing the shoes on a TLS brake where the brake cams are operated by a rod connecting a single lever pulled by a cable to the second lever. Anyone who has tried to set up the previous BSA/Triumph TLS brake will know that this is a fiddly job needing at least three hands to do it properly, and if it is not done correctly will seriously compromise the performance of the brake.

However, as good as this aspect of the design was, it was overshadowed by a fundamental problem in the operating mechanism. A Bowden cable is designed to guide an inner cable from one fixed point (the handlebar lever) to another (the cable stop on the brake plate) – the outer should act only as a guide. However, the new BSA design relied on the cable both to guide the inner cable and to act as an end stop. A Bowden cable outer is essentially a close-wound spring, and can compress and reduce in length. This is not a problem in a conventional brake where the cable outer is simply guiding the cable from the lever to the brake, because the outer is subject to little (if any) compressive force, as the cable inner is pulling between and against two fixed points. In the Umberslade BSA brake, pulling on the brake lever presses the brake shoes against the brake drum, but will also compress the outer cable, reducing the force available to be converted into braking. BSA did appear to have taken this effect into account by providing a large diameter cable, much more robust than any that had been used previously. In normal use, correctly set up and using the heavyweight cable, the BSA brake was pretty good.

Contemporary road tests show reasonable stopping distances from 30mph, but identified that heavy use led to the brake fading, despite the large air scoop on the front of the brake plate. A secondary problem was water ingress. If a bike was left on its side stand, rainwater collected in the brake because of inadequate sealing. This could result in some interesting braking characteristics, from the brake not working at all when drenched, through to excessive grabbiness at low speeds when it began to dry out – exactly what you don't want a brake to do when the roads are wet! The problem was caused by the fact that the brake back plate was on the opposite side to the side stand, leaning the bike such that water could get in but not drain out. The ultimate solution appears to be the fitting of a disc brake from a later 650 or 750 Triumph! Why BSA spent so much time and effort in producing a new drum brake when it should have been developing a disc is lost in the mists of time.

Wheels

The range started with 18in diameter wheels front and rear and then went through a bewildering flurry of changes in the mid 1960s, finally settling down as the range contracted in the late 1960s. Initially, Star Twins were fitted with 3.25 × 18 front and 3.50 × 18 rear tyres, with WM2 width rims. In 1965 the Lightning and Cyclone introduced 3.25 × 19in front and 3.50 × 19 rear wheels and tyres, still with WM2 width rims. In 1966, the Royal Star had 3.25 × 19 front and 3.50 × 19 rear; the Wasp and Hornet had 3.50 × 19 front and 4.00 × 18 rear; the Lightning and Thunderbolt had 3.25 × 19 front and 3.50 × 19 rear; and finally the Spitfire Mk II had 3.25 × 19 front and 4.00 × 18 rear. WM2 rims were still specified, except for the models with 4.00 section rear tyres, which had rear rims of WM3 width specified. Things started to settle down in 1967 with the whole range standardizing on 19in diameter front wheels with WM2 rim, and 18in diameter rear wheels with WM3 rims. These sizes then continued unchanged into the 1971 range.

The original fitment full-width hubs were made from high-grade cast iron, and were designed to enable straight pull spokes to be used. This design made for stronger, more rigid wheels, but due to the material used there was a weight problem. The rear wheel fitted to the original Star models was not described by BSA as quickly detachable, but was designed to enable the wheel to be removed without disturbing the chain or rear brake adjustment.

The brake was positioned on the timing side, and was operated via the shaft running through the swinging arm spindle. To take the wheel out, the four bolts that fixed the sprocket to the hub were removed, then the rear brake rod was released and finally the axle unscrewed. The wheel could then be removed, leaving the sprocket and its carrier still fixed to the swinging arm. This rather clumsy mechanism was replaced from 1965 (with the introduction of the Lightning) and throughout the whole range in 1966 by the famous BSA 'crinkle' hub, a true QD design.

The original 1962 rear hub was attached to the rear sprocket by four bolts and the wheel spindle.

This design had the rear brake and sprocket combined as a unit which bolted to the left-hand (drive) side of the swinging arm on a stub axle. The rear brake was operated by rod, with a conventional pivot for the pedal bolted to the frame below the swinging arm spindle. The wheel was mounted on to this sprocket and brake unit through a set of splines, and was retained by the rear wheel spindle, which bolted into the stub axle. Removal of the rear wheel simply meant undoing the spindle, removing a spacer and pulling the wheel off of the spline – a truly simple and elegant solution that needed no spanners, only a tommy bar to execute. The 1965 bikes also had the speedometer driven from the gearbox, so there was no speedometer drive to worry about, although the speedometer drive was moved to the right-hand side of the rear wheel spindle in 1966. This meant that the drive had to be removed or the speedometer cable disconnected before the wheel could be released. The design of the crinkle hub also meant that, as on the original full-width hubs, the spokes were straight with a direct line from the drillings in the rim to hub, making for a strong and rigid wheel, which was easy to build and adjust, easy to remove if getting a puncture.

The front wheels fitted to the range broadly followed the same saga as the rear. Initially, the Star's front wheel was secured by bolted-on fork end caps, which held each side of the wheel

spindle of the full-width hub. A slot in the fork leg located the brake back plate. This wheel was complemented on the Lightning models in 1965 by the 8in half-width brake, which had a screw-in spindle, which could be operated by a tommy bar, and was fixed by a pinch bolt on the left-hand fork leg. The torque arm also was bolted on to the brake plate and needed more spanner work to remove. This brake was fitted across the range from 1966, except for the Spitfire, which had the Gold Star 190mm full-width hub. However, this brake had the same type of fixings as the 8in half-width hub, with a push-in spindle and bolt-on torque arm allowing for common fork legs across the range.

The introduction of the Triumph type TLS brake in 1968 reverted to the original type of fitting with bolt-on fork caps (two bolts per cap) and the brake back plate locating in a slot in the fork leg. The final conical hub had bolt on fork caps with four nuts and studs. These were supposed to provide rigidity to the forks by clamping the wheel spindle firmly, as the tops of the fork sliders had no real bracing, only the rubber-mounted wire mudguard stays. However, this was not very successful and the forks were prone to flexing. Later Triumphs using the same forks replaced the wire stays with a stronger bridge piece, but by then the BSAs were no longer in production. A stud on the brake plate which engaged in a lug on the fork leg was used

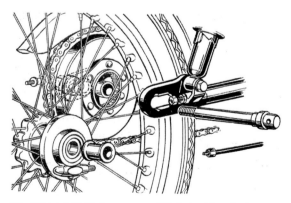

The BSA 'crinkle' hub was a true QD design. The wheel was removed after extracting the spindle, leaving the chain and brake undisturbed.

The unit twin range was introduced in 1962 with this cheerful brochure. BSA was obviously pleased with the 'twins' theme: two new bikes and twin cylinders, so get a set of twins to promote them – very 1950s in appearance.

By 1964 the twins were established as the top-of-the-range bikes. So they appear on the cover of the brochure, which now looks very 1960s.

ABOVE: For the 1968 American market, BSA was pushing the lifestyle. Here Spitfire Mk IV *is displayed with its owners, again the top of the range at the time.*

For the final year, 1972, BSA ignored the top-of-the-range Rocket 3, and put this image of a Lightning on the cover of its brochure. It was BSA who remov the top of the rider's head, but it is a superb, moody shot all the same.

BELOW: Jeremy Scott's 1962 A65 is reasonably original, with only the seat, mudguards, silencers and front brake non-standard. It gives a good impression a working bike.

There are a large number of unit twins out and about in the UK. The following pictures were taken in May 2003 at the Fleet Lions Run. This is a nice 1969–70 specification Thunderbolt.

This looks like an early Lightning, with dropped-yoke forks, early tank and filler cap and sidepanels. Closer inspection shows Concentric carbs and later seat. Altogether a nice bike.

This is a Firebird Scrambler of 1969–70. Good looks came as standard and the high-level exhaust system with two silencers makes an impressive sight on the drive side.

This oil-in-frame Firebird Scrambler from 1971 shows the slim lines inherent in the design of the A65.

LEFT: This standard early Star with its nacelle and valanced mudguards contrasts with the 1965–66 A65 in the Rocket style behind.

TOP LEFT: *This early Hornet (or is it a Cyclone/Wasp?) displays some concessions to road use, with its siamesed exhaust system, Gold Star-type silencer and number plate.*

ABOVE: *The 1972 home-market brochure pictures of the Lightning (top) and Thunderbird show the adoption of the black frame and the large 'breadbin'-style tank.*

ABOVE: *This mid-60s Lightning, possibly a Clubman, has all the café racer accessories – the humped seat, clip-on handlebars, Gold Star-type headlamp fixings and reverse-cone meggas. All in all a fine example of the café racers' art, but still retaining the classic BSA look.*

As bought, the restoration project 1965 A65 was complete but looking a bit sorry for itself. While mainly in one piece, the bike was found to be loosely assembled when the restoration commenced.

Chris Burrell's 1972 Firebird Scrambler, with its black frame, is probably the best-looking of the oil-in-frame models.

BELOW: The results of the restoration speak for themselves. While not standard, the Spitfire style tank and later side panels in solid red really present a striking image.

From the other side, the bike exudes performance. Both pictures were taken in February 2004.

BELOW: This is what the 1965 brochure image of the Lightning shows. The much retouched image shows the non-humped seat and the quick-release filler cap on the fuel tank that are carried over from the Rocket. Flamboyant red was an option.

500 Cyclone
650 Lightning

New two carburetter high performance twins

Fresh from a successful conquest of the American market come these sparkling new twins. We've even retained the American names—Lightning for the 650, Cyclone for the 500. High compression pistons, special camshaft, two monobloc carburetters with cylindrical air cleaners, twin-mounted speedometer and tachometer, chromium plated headlamp, fork covers, mudguards and fuel tank are just some of the features to make these models the undoubted leaders in their class. As for performance, it's breathtaking—coupled of course with the traditional BSA standards of braking, steering and handling.

Speed . Sparkle . Stamina

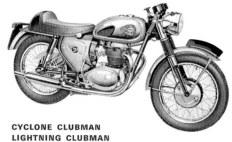

CYCLONE CLUBMAN
LIGHTNING CLUBMAN

For production sports model racing both the Lightning and Cyclone may be specified (at a small additional charge) with rear mounted footrests brake pedal and gearchange, racing seat, special silencer and downswept handlebars, as shown in this photograph.

Model A65L

BSA

This rare period colour shot shows a 1963 A65 Rocket. The bike is virtually standard, with only the luggage rack and handlebar mirror fitted deviating from the factory specification.

BELOW: This 1968 model year brochure has photos of the bikes which have not been heavily retouched. The lifestyle marketing is kicking in with the stylized yachtsmen!

650 c.c. Thunderbolt A65T

The 650 c.c. Thunderbolt the epitome of power and reliability. Surging power, vivid acceleration and flexibility combine with steering and suspension that are both light and responsive. This is the touring model with sports performance. Special features included as standard are chrome plated blade-type mud guards, new style petrol tank with sports "snap" filler, rubber gaitered front forks, sports headlamp and race style safety dual seat. Colour finish is Black and Chrome.

650 c.c. Lightning A65L

A sports model with a pedigree feel and appeal. Speed equipped. Matched rubber mounted speedo and tachometer, twin leading shoe front brake and special two way front fork damping. All this and a lot more make this a machine in a million—the envy of other road users—very fast but easy to handle and ultra reliable under all conditions. Finished in Flamboyant Red, Chrome and polished alloy.

The successful end of a restoration with the bike on the road is always a gratifying time.

The oil-in-frame rear brake was housed in a conical alloy hub, matching the front in style. It was not a QD design.

to locate the brake back plate. It was then positively fixed in position by screwing on a nut and thick washer.

Tinwear

As with any motorcycle of this period, the tinwear, comprising the petrol tank, oil tank, side panels and mudguards, defined the overall styling of the unit twin range. While any comments on appearance are subjective, it is true to say that during the model's life, the appearance ranged from dumpy and staid, to something approaching Triumph's leanness. However, it is also true to say that the range always managed to maintain a distinct BSA family appearance. Dominant was the petrol tank, and apart from the Spitfire, the Hornet and Firebird Scrambler models, this was

the classic BSA oval shape, with chromed side panels and a BSA logo in a star badge – usually pear-shaped, except for the early US export models that had round ones.

The petrol tank had the famous BSA centre bolt fixing. The tank sat on a pair of U-shaped rubber bushes, and was fixed in position by a vertical stud that was passed through a rubber bush held in a 1in diameter hole in the centre of the tank. A further fitting strap was fixed by two studs on the front of the tank to prevent the tank splitting and as an 'anti-sway' device. On the pre oil-in-frame models, this fitting was also rubber-mounted on to a lug on the frame to provide a more positive fixing. On the original Star models, the petrol tank, mudguards and side panels were all made from steel pressings.

The initial Star models were the most rounded

The 'generic' BSA tank fitted to the Unit Twins – this is from a 1968 US model – featured chrome side panels and the pear-shaped BSA badges. UK versions were larger and earlier versions had rubber knee grips.

BELOW: The nacelle and associated pressings styled the front end.

and staid – they were basically softly tuned tourers, and the large side panels, headlamp nacelle and valanced mudguards, all painted, emphasized this usage.

The side panels concealed the oil tank and toolbox on the left-hand side and the battery carrier on the right.

The toolbox started off as a compartment behind the oil tank formed of a steel pressing with a plate affixed to the front on the lower half

to retain a tool roll, which was superseded the following year with an open pressing with a leather-look zipped bag fixed in it to carry the tools.

The optional fully enclosed chaincase added to the sensible and serious image, but with the move towards an increasingly sporty look was dropped from the options list in 1966. It was never a listed option on the sportier Rocket, Cyclone or Lightning. The sporting models,

The tool kit was situated behind the oil tank. Early models had a plate across the bottom of the box to retain a tool roll.

model, and was relocated at the base of the steering head, allowing a slimmer headlamp shell to be used. The Spitfire models gained glass-fibre racing-styled tanks – either a large red 5gal (23l) endurance racing-style with heavily scalloped knee grips, or a small 2gal enduro style, while the Lightning and Thunderbolt models kept the trademark BSA oval chromed tank in large or small sizes. The final incarnation of the model range, the oil-in-frame models of 1971, had minimal chromed mudguards giving little weather protection, a choice of small (2½gal/11l) or large (4gal/18l) painted steel petrol tanks and chromed headlamps on wire stays. The side panels were made up from two pieces – a small steel triangular piece to the rear, and a stylized plastic cover with fake louvres for the air filters.

starting with the Rocket, started to dispel the sensible image in the 1964 model year. The mudguards lost the valance and were chromed, and the headlamp was separate and mounted on chromed brackets – although the headlamp shell itself was painted black and quite bulbous as it still carried the ammeter, light and ignition switches.

Both of these styling features slimmed down the appearance a surprising amount. This trend continued with the sporting models, with the Lightning gaining slightly smaller glass-fibre side panels (although reverting to metal in 1968) to clear the separate air cleaners fitted to the twin carburettors, and a slimmer chrome headlamp shell lightening the appearance even more.

The ignition switch was replaced on all models in 1966 with a proper key-operated

Later models had a leather-look zipped bag fixed into the tool carrier, into which tools could be stored.

The 1964 Rocket and 1965 Lightning models introduced a separate headlamp and instruments. While larger than the later models, this helped to slim down the appearance.

From 1966 a smaller, bullet-shaped headlamp was used. This is shown here on a 1969 Thunderbolt.

Electrics

The electrics fitted to the range in 1962 were innovative for the time and were also used on the smaller BSA four-stroke singles (the 250cc C15 and 350cc B40) lower down the BSA range of the early 1960s. As described above, Lucas had introduced an AC alternator-based system, which was substantially cheaper to produce than a dynamo and magneto, and demand for separate dynamos and magnetos was waning. The unit twins exploited this new system, with a crankshaft-mounted AC alternator placed in the primary chaincase, which was used to generate 6V AC current. This was converted to 6V DC using a solid-state diode-based full wave rectifier, and the current used to charge a 6V battery, mounted under the seat. The battery was then used to power the lights, horn and coil ignition.

There was no 'active' current regulation on the 6V system. The output of the alternator was switched in through the combined ignition and light switch in three increments. The ignition-only position connected two out of the six alternator coils, giving one-third of the output. Turning on the sidelights switched in another two alternator coils, giving two-thirds of the available output, and turning on the ignition and main lights switched in all six coils, giving the full output of the alternator. Finally, there was an 'emergency' position on the ignition switch, which switched in all six of the alternator coils to facilitate starting if the battery was flat. Whether this 'emergency' system ever worked was a moot point. While this type of system was fairly common at the time, the fact remains that it was crude, ineffective and unreliable. Worse, it required unnecessarily complicated wiring and switchgear, with lots of connectors, so was without any of the benefits of simplicity. The lack of voltage regulation could lead to over-charging and a boiled-dry battery, for example during a long, fast ride, and undercharging, for example while riding slowly in heavy traffic. The good things about the system were that it was reasonably cheap and it worked adequately in most situations, when in good condition.

Thus, the system effectively presented to the rider the worst of both worlds, and it is this type of 6V system that led to the poor reputation of

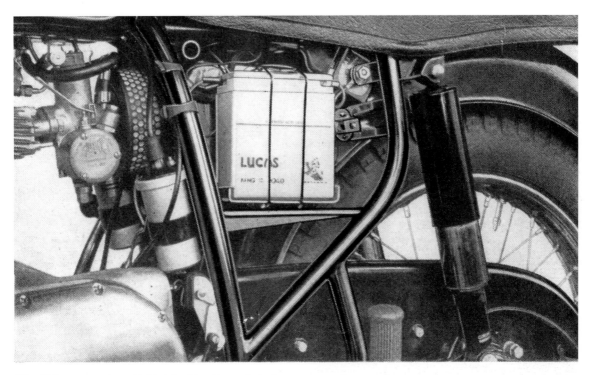

The 6V battery was situated behind the drive-side panel. A wire strap was used to secure it.

British bikes for electrical reliability. While in good repair the system would work adequately, add in a dash of poor maintenance, corrosion, wear in the switchgear and connectors, and a battery past its best, and the die was cast.

Once the battery was flat, the bike would not easily start or run. This skinflint approach to battery and coil electrical systems was in marked contrast to the relatively reliable dynamo/magneto systems previously offered.

The only good point of the whole electrical system was that the ignition system was a contact breaker point and coil-based system from the inception of the model, resulting in easy starting as long as the battery held enough juice. The BSA design team declined to follow contemporary coil ignition design practices, placing a single or two sets of contact breaker points in a distributor driven from a skew gear. Instead, the team provided twin contact breaker points and a mechanical advance/retard unit in the timing case, driven from the camshaft drive idler gear

which ran at half engine speed. While this design decision not to use a distributor was made purely on cost grounds, avoiding the need for both a distributor and the associated separate drive mechanism, it did lead the way that the Triumph twin would go. Many mourned the demise of the magneto, as it did not rely on the battery condition to provide sparks – but it was expensive, heavier and more complicated than the coil system. Provision for stroboscopic timing using a pointer in the primary chaincase and timing mark on the alternator stator was introduced in 1967. The initial A50s and A65s were equipped with Lucas 4CA contact breaker points and back plate.

This set-up had one major flaw, in that the assembly did not allow for individual timing of both cylinders. The only way this could be achieved was by altering the contact breaker gap, which required a degree of skill and care to set up accurately. The problem was that in altering the contact breaker gap from the recommended

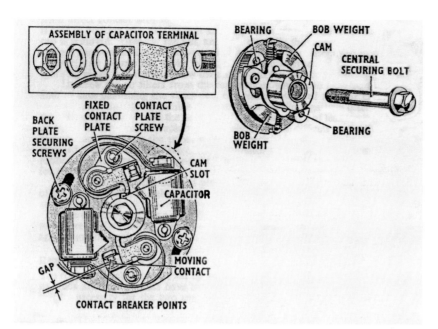

The original contact breaker points fitted were the Lucas 4CA. These lacked provision for independent timing of cylinders. Note the mechanical advance/retard unit.

The Ignition Woes of the Mid 1960s

In the 1965–66 model year a major problem arose with the twins – there was a spate of mechanical problems that appeared initially to be overheating, with results that included seizures, top-end problems and severe piston damage. This dented BSA's reputation for reliability quite badly. Interestingly, the issue was not mentioned in road tests at the time, but was referred to in tests on the twins in the following year by *Cycle* and *Cycle World* in the US. The problem was summed up pretty accurately by Cycle: '. . . last year a lot of BSAs expired in untidy fashion. Pistons collapsed, valves jammed and spark plugs fried themselves into oblivion. Not on all BSAs; many ran without giving their owners a bit of trouble. The rest just about drove BSA's engineers and their owners right out of their respective minds.'

The problem was particularly obscure and took a lot of time and effort from both sides of the Atlantic to cure. Eventually, the problem was traced to the profile of the ignition system's contact breaker cam, which was causing the contact breakers to bounce which generated a rogue spark, which then caused pre-ignition and consequential damage. The whole episode cost BSA a lot both in terms of money in warranty claims and in replacing the contact breaker points cam on every machine manufactured.

15 thou to get the timing right on a cylinder you had to alter the contact breaker point gap, resulting in either a correct gap and incorrect timing, or more commonly a compromise between the two settings. This was not seen as a problem with the early, softly tuned models, but as the engine unit was tuned, ignition timing became more critical and the weakness in the design resulted in, at the least, a loss of performance and at worst holed pistons.

The 4CA contact breakers and their associated back plate were superseded for 1968 by the Lucas 6CA contact breakers and back plate, which allowed the relative position of each set of contact breakers to be adjusted independently. This was achieved by mounting each set of contact breakers on a separate platform on the back plate, which enabled each contact breaker assembly to be moved radially independently of each other. While this meant that both the timing and the contact breaker point gap for each cylinder could be precisely set up, the timing process was even more complex than before, and still needed real skill and care to ensure an accurate setting – but the advantage

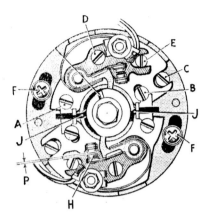

From 1968, the Lucas 6CA points were fitted. These had provision for individually adjusting the timing of each cylinder.

was that the timing could be set up to be spot-on for both cylinders.

An electrical innovation was introduced for the 1964 model year in the form of an 'energy transfer' ignition system. The objective of this system was to provide battery-less operation of the ignition system for the US market off-road models – the 500cc Cyclone and 650cc Spitfire Hornet. The system comprised a special alternator (Lucas Type RM19ET), coils (Lucas 3ET), condensers (Lucas No. 54441582) and contact breaker (Lucas 4CA.ET). The alternator was designed to provide a correctly timed pulse of AC electricity directly to the coils via the contact breaker points, which would then produce the spark for the plugs. The system appeared to

The zener diode heat sink was located in the airflow under the bottom yoke. The ignition switch was also located here in 1966 models.

work well, with contemporary road tests commenting on easy starting and good running.

The 6V system was discarded with the advent of 12V electrical systems – but not as rapidly as it should have been. A 12V system was originally offered as an option in 1964, but was only standardized in 1965 and even then was utilizing twin 6V batteries in series, mounted behind the left-hand side panel. A single 12V battery didn't replace the two linked 6V batteries until 1967.

The 12V system used a zener diode for current regulation. This was an efficient and simple system that resulted in much simpler wiring and switchgear than the 6V system.

The zener diode regulated the system by sensing the system voltage and hence the condition of the battery. If the battery charge state was low, its voltage would be low and the diode allowed the full output of the alternator to be directed into the battery to charge it. As the battery achieved full charge, the voltage of the system rose, and the zener diode would then 'dump' excess energy to earth. This energy was converted into heat – hence the need for a large heat sink. The heat sink was originally placed under the seat, but was moved to a position under the bottom fork yoke, where it got plenty of cooling air in 1968. The system was self-regulating, with no moving parts, was very simple to wire with no complex switches, and was very reliable. The main source of problems with this system was when the heat sink could not lose the heat generated by the diode quickly enough – for example if the airflow around it was not sufficient. This resulted in a burnt-out diode which could fail open circuit, resulting in a blown fuse or a closed circuit and no charge for the battery. While a blown fuse would stop the bike, it could still be got to run by disconnecting the diode and replacing the fuse. The full output of the alternator was then put into the battery with no regulation, so was advisable to run with the lights on and not go too far, as eventually the battery would be boiled dry. Exactly the same 12V system was used by Triumph and all other British manufacturers. The 12V system offered by BSA had three major

advantages over the previous 6V system – it was simple, reliable and cheap.

A further innovation of the 12V system was the provision for the fitting of a capacitor. This electronic component was designed to store a charge for a brief period of time and then discharge it on demand. Hence it could be used to replace a battery – it would store enough charge from the alternator to power the ignition system. It had two purposes – it could run the bike's ignition system if the battery was flat (or indeed dead), and it could also allow the bike to be run without a battery. So if someone was brave and strong enough to take a Firebird Scrambler off-road, the battery could be removed completely, saving weight, and removing the possibility of damage from spilt battery acid if the bike was dropped.

At the start of the model line in 1962, the two switches for lights and ignition were mounted on the left-hand side in the nacelle.

The nacelle carried all the instruments and the switches. This 1962 model has had a key-operated switch added as an additional security measure.

The speedometer occupied the centre of the nacelle, with an ammeter in the right-hand side. Both switches were reasonably easy to see and get at when moving, unlike the ammeter, although the ignition switch was the standard Lucas offering of the time, which offered minimal security – a screwdriver could be used to operate it. The nacelle was replaced on the sportier models by a separate headlamp supported by chromed 'ears', starting with the Rocket of 1964 with ignition and light switches either side of a centrally mounted ammeter. This assembly was also used on the Lightning in 1965 and on all models when the nacelle was finally dropped in 1966. Later models had two warning lights mounted in the headlamp (confusingly coloured blue for oil pressure and red for headlamp main beam) either side of the ammeter. From 1966 the ignition switch, with a proper key to operate it, was conveniently positioned on the frame, at the front left-hand side of the steering head lug, just ahead of the petrol tank rather than in the headlamp. A circular Wipac Ducon combination dip switch and horn button were placed on the left-hand handlebar from the introduction in 1962.

Ignition coils were positioned behind and below the carburettors, with the HT lead exiting vertically – which could lead to water shorting out the leads in heavy rain. The electrical system then remained virtually unchanged in both design and layout through to the introduction of the Umberslade oil-in-frame models in 1971.

The Wipac Ducon or Tricon switch was one of the better-looking handlebar switches available to manufacturers. It was fitted as standard to the range from 1962–70.

Rear lighting started with a traditional pressed steel light and number plate assembly, supporting a combined rectangular light and reflector (Lucas model type 564). This was superseded in the UK in 1967 by a handsome cast alloy assembly, already used for the 1966 US market models, which utilized the new Lucas standard design of rear light (model type 679 or the 'Tit'), and separate brackets for the number plate. The cast alloy lamp carrier was also used on the contemporary Triumph twins, and was generally considered to be the best-looking rear light used by BSA and Triumph. This unit was replaced in 1968 with a larger alloy carrier, with triangular red reflectors incorporated on each side to meet US regulations.

The 1971 oil-in-frame models retained the 12V system and still used the zener diode to provide voltage regulation. This component was moved to a new position under the seat and used the new large alloy air cleaner housing as a heat sink, a system that worked well.

The electrical system introduced a number of innovations aimed at both meeting legislation and bringing the range in line with the management's perception of the competition. Lucas still produced all the electrics, and the most noticeable feature of the new system was the flashing indicators, round amber lights mounted on chrome bodies and stalks front and rear. These required additional switchgear to operate and BSA took the opportunity to update this aspect

For 1971, the main electrical components were positioned on a rubber mounted plate under the hinged seat. Note the condenser pack between the vertically mounted coils and the ignition switch in the side panel.

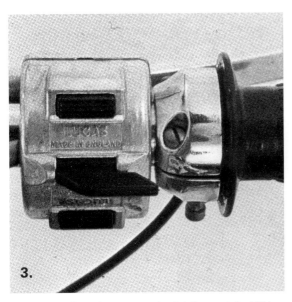

3.

Lucas eventually made an integrated switch/lever unit in 1971 to compete with the Japanese. While it was a step in the right direction, its ergonomics were not ideal.

side to side action, the switches being unmarked and the toggles used looking flimsy. Riders getting used to a new bike very quickly overcame most of these – and the switches actually proved to be pretty robust in use. While they were possibly not the most ergonomic (certainly for small-handed people), they were close to what the Japanese were doing at the time.

The chromed headlamp on the 1971 year onwards was supported in rubber-mounted wire stays, and had green (main beam), red (oil pressure) and amber (indicators) warning lights placed in the rear edge of the headlamp shell, the back of which was flattened. There was a rotating light switch on the top of the headlamp shell, which switched between pilot and dip/main lights. While the Thunderbolt and Lightning

of the range through adopting Japanese-style cast aluminium switch assemblies.

These were designed and manufactured by Lucas and incorporated high-quality alloy control levers with built-in cable adjusters – definitely more up-market than the pressed steel ones previously employed. The switch assemblies had three functions each – a central toggle switch and a rectangular push button above and below the toggle. The toggle switch could have two or three positions – the dip and main beam switch on the left-hand bar having two positions, and the indicator switch on the right-hand side three. The two push buttons on the left-hand bar operated the horn, and, a new feature, a headlamp main beam flasher. On the right-hand side, the lower push button provided another new feature, an engine cut-out function, and the top one had no function. Speculation was that this was for the electric start . . .

The switches came in for a lot of criticism, including the edges of the alloy control levers being too sharp and digging into riders' fingers, the indicator switch having an up/down movement (just like a car indicator stalk) rather than a

The rear light carrier was nicknamed 'the gargoyle'. The rear indicators on short stalks were carried on the unit.

Positioning of the ignition switch on the rear of the timing-side panel was not good ergonomics, especially as the switch also controlled the lights. It was also easy for a pillion passenger to break the key off when mounting the machine.

both sported a 7in diameter unit, the Firebird Scrambler made do with a 6in unit – which looked the part on a street scrambler, but did not provide as much forward light as the larger unit.

The rear light lens and reflector was the Lucas 679 'Tit' type as before, but was mounted on a pressed steel assembly which was nicknamed 'the gargoyle' for its poor appearance. The assembly also carried the rear indicators.

The ignition system remained the same as before, although the coils, condensers and, when fitted, the capacitor were mounted vertically under the hinged seat, as was the battery.

One retrograde step was the repositioning of the key-operated switch on the rear of the right-hand side panel. The switch was multi-functional and controlled the lights as well as the ignition.

So the rider had to reach behind his or her right leg to turn on the ignition, and, probably more dangerously, had to fumble down there to turn the lights on. This may have simplified the wiring harness design, but was poorly thought out and obviously not designed by a motor-cyclist.

Instruments

As was the custom of the day, instrumentation was basic but informative. Initially, the Star Twins were provided with a Smith's chronometric speedometer and an ammeter – hence the rider could see how fast he or she was going, and, with a certain amount of interpretation of the amme-ter's reading, how much longer the engine would keep going until the battery was discharged! The speedometer and ammeter were both housed within the nacelle. The chronometric speedo-meter fitted to the earlier machines included a trip meter, and the face was not the traditional black, but was a light grey/blue – very similar in colour and appearance to the later magnetic instruments. During the 1964 model year, the chronometric speedometer was replaced with the cheaper Smith's magnetic instrument.

The first bikes were equipped with a Smith's chronometric speedometer. Note also the ammeter in the nacelle, angled away from the rider's field of view.

The early engines had the speedometer driven from the inner timing cover. An alloy disc that identified the speedometer drive ratio (in this case 7:10) was fixed to the cover.

The cheaper Smith's magnetic instruments were introduced during the 1964 model year. Here they are individually mounted in metal pods.

The speedometer was initially driven from the gearbox, with the cable drive protruding out of the middle bottom of the inner timing cover. This did result in a rather sharp curve in the cable needed to miss the frame and the exhaust pipe mounting bracket. On these bikes, BSA provided a small disc on the top right-hand face of the gearbox, which had the number of teeth of the gears of the speedometer drive (for example, 8:12 or 7:12) and hence the speedometer drive ratio.

BSA offered five different pairs of drive gears to account for variations in wheel and tyre size and overall gearing. The drive for the speedometer was relocated to the timing side of the rear wheel during the 1966 model year, and remained there until the demise of the range in 1972.

The 1964 A65R Rocket was the first in the range to have the optional extra of a tachometer. At the start of the 1964 model year both instruments were Smith's chronometric type (as illustrated in a January 1964 road test by *Motor Cycle*), with traditional black faces, but later on in the model year both were changed to the cheaper and possibly less robust and accurate

The instruments were mounted on an alloy plate from 1965, and rubber pods superseded the metal pods in 1967 initially only on the US specification models. This is a 1969 model with the later mounting plate and rubber cups.

magnetic type. The magnetic instruments were rubber-mounted in round metal pods to provide insulation from vibration.

Initially, the speedometer and tachometer in their pods were individually mounted on the fork tube top nuts on small triangular mounts, but this arrangement was quickly superseded by mounting the two pods on a single cast alloy plate, which was in turn bolted on the fork top yoke. This arrangement was carried over to the Lightning and Spitfire models. For 1968, the metal pod was superseded by an all-rubber cup, which totally enclosed the instrument and was bolted directly on to the alloy mounting bracket.

The Thunderbolt only had a speedometer, and this was centrally mounted using a single metal pod on the fork top yoke up till 1967, when it

was superseded by a single rubber cup.

The Umberslade redesign of the frame for the 1971 model year resulted in the speedometer and tachometer being mounted in individual rubber pods, which were in turn fixed to the fork top nuts by chromed rings – reminiscent of the method of mounting the dual instruments in 1965. Both instruments were black-faced with white numbers and red needles introduced the previous year. The Thunderbolt still only had a speedometer, mounted on the right-hand side fork yoke top nut, giving a lop-sided appearance – a retrograde step from the centrally mounted instrument of the pre oil-in-frame model. The ammeter remained in the headlamp until the introduction of the 1971 model, when it was deleted.

Summary

The development of the range followed a path of gentle evolution, with changes usually being introduced on the sporting models, then being reflected the following year throughout the range. This evolutionary approach worked well, with noticeable improvements being made to the range year on year, and with new sporting flagships holding the fort against rivals – especially Triumph! This approach was turned on its head with the replacement of the range's running gear in 1971, with the introduction of the oil-in-frame models. This expensive opera- tion can be seen with hindsight to have been a major mistake. The company should have spent the money on developing a range of replace- ment engines, for both the A65 and the Triumph twin, which were showing their age against the Japanese opposition and modern road condi- tions. These replacement engines could have been accommodated in the existing running gear, which still had better handling and road holding than the competition. Basically, the company fixed the bit that wasn't broken, and didn't fix the bit that was!

Finally, the instruments were mounted on the fork top nuts on individual rubber pods. Note the 6in headlamp on this 1971 Firebird – the Thunderbolt and Lightning both had 7in units.

4 Competition History

Introduction

With its 3½hp model firmly established, and proving to be reliable and a good performer, BSA started to enter the competition world during 1913. Spurred on by the success of Ken Holden winning the first race he was entered in at the Brooklands track in Surrey in early 1913, a team of seven 3½hp machines was entered in the June TT Races on the Isle of Man. The race was a two-day, two-stage event, but by the end of the second stage only one BSA rider was still competing, and he (Irishman R. Carey) eventually finished in a lowly seventeenth place. Better results were achieved in the French Grand Prix in July 1913, with BSA achieving a third place. During 1913 BSA also started competing in six-day events and reliability trials. Competition was suspended during the 1914–18 war, and resumed thereafter. The turning point for road competition was the 1921 TT Races – BSA had not had any machines ready for the 1920 races, but had been developing state of the art 500cc four-valve alloy head machines with a duplex frame to contest the 1921 season. Much publicity was generated in the press at the time, with predictions that the BSA should carry all before it. All six of the machines entered in the race failed to finish, all retiring with 'engine trouble'. As a result of the adverse publicity, the factory decided not to pursue international road racing for many years.

This did not preclude the factory from gaining a great deal of competition success – both on the road and on the rough. On the road, the Gold Star singles and A7s twins took the first five places in the 1954 US National Motorcycle Championship at Daytona, while at home the Gold Star singles dominated the Clubman's TT race series of 1947 to 1956. In the series, BSA won nearly twice as many times as any other manufacturer in the series, and dominated the event to such an extent that the series was ended in 1956.

Off-road, the Gold Star gained many motocross successes, including many ACU 500 championships, and Jeff Smith, riding the unit single 500cc motocross bikes, gained British and World Motocross championships in 1964 and 1965, and further national championships in 1967, 68 and 69.

However, in competition the A50 and A65 were used mainly in a piecemeal and unofficial capacity by the works. The twins were too big and heavy to be competitive off-road, and with the management still opposed to international road racing, the unit twins only competed in production racing and sidecar racing with the exception of the A50 being used to compete in the US at Daytona to try to emulate the successes of 1954. They consequently had only limited resources available to develop them in road-racing roles, and even then improvements made to the engines for racing did not find their way into production models. The A50 was further disadvantaged by being a sleeved-down 650, while its main competitor, the 500cc unit Triumph, was a bored-out 350cc, and was lighter and more agile. However, despite these handicaps the unit twins did not disgrace themselves in competition, and certainly found some niches where considerable success was achieved.

The 1962 International Six-Day Trial

In the 1962 ISDT held in Garmisch-Partenkirchen in West Germany, Johnny Harris rode a modified A50 as part of the British Trophy team, and won an individual Gold Medal. In common with many of the successful BSA sportsmen of the time, John Harris worked in the BSA comp shop from 1958–63, and won two Gold Medals in the ISDTs – in 1961, at Llandrindrod Wells, Wales, and in 1962 in West Germany on the A50. In the 1962 event, Czechoslovakia won the Trophy, and Germany won the Silver Vase.

The BSA A50 he rode had few modifications from standard, mainly intended to take into account the on/off road aspects of the competition. The engine and gearbox were almost completely standard, but the compression ratio was raised to 8.5:1 and the gearing was lower. The exhaust was a high-level, siamesed system that was routed inside the main frame tubes under the oil tank, and was attached to a short C15 competition silencer. The frame was the standard item, but with a steel sump guard and Gold Star type forks and wheels – giving the true QD rear, and the 8in half-width hub at the front. The C15 Competition model also supplied the seat, headlamp and handlebar, while an alloy fuel tank and twin 6V batteries finished the specification.

It was reported at the time that a road speed of 90mph (145km/h) could be achieved by the bike in full ISDT trim – which was pretty close to that achieved by the standard road-going A50, and is all the more outstanding bearing in mind the lower off-road gearing and higher handlebars. The BSA works did not capitalize on this single victory with the A50, and went on to use B40 and B44 derivatives for the following years – with some success. This was likely due to the weight of the A50 when compared with the unit singles – the singles were probably 50 to 100lb (23 to 45kg) lighter than the A50, a significant issue on a six-day trial.

Steve Harris, of the Hertfordshire UK based frame makers of the same name campaigned this A65 Spitfire production racer during the 1967 and 1968 seasons.

John Cooper won the production machine race in the 1966 Hutchinson 100 race at Brands Hatch on this Spitfire production racer.

Tony Smith on his works Lightning during the 1968 500-mile production race at Brands Hatch. The BSA finished 4th in the 750cc class.

Solo – Production Racing and Daytona

As a solo racing machine the unit twin formed the basis for two main road race types. In the UK the A65 was used by a number of riders in 650cc production racer events throughout the 1960s. In the US, between 1966 and 1968, BSA entered a works sponsored and developed team of heavily modified A50s in the prestigious Daytona 200 races.

The first significant race success for a solo A65 was achieved in August 1965, when Mike Hailwood, riding a works-prepared production A65L Lightning, won the Production Machine Race in the Hutchinson 100 event at Silverstone.

In the event, he beat famous racers Phil Read and Percy Tait, both mounted on 650cc Triumphs, and achieved a fastest lap time of over 85mph (137km/h). The bike did have a frame with a different steering head angle to the production models. Famously, at the same meeting Hailwood also won the 500cc race on his MV 4 cylinder machine and the 350cc race on an AJS – winning three races on one day on a single, a twin and a four. This win was mirrored in the 1966 event, which was staged at Brands Hatch. There, John 'Moon Eyes' Cooper won the event on a production BSA A65S Spitfire at 80.12mph (128.91km/h).

The 650cc twin was used extensively in production racing by private entrants, who were

Even BSA's brochures played down the competition aspects of the Unit Twins, preferring to portray the bikes in social settings! This is a picture of a 1968 US specification Lightning from the US brochure.

The A65 based Kirby-BSA Sidecar outfit enjoyed considerable success in the 1960s, including winning the 750cc class in the Isle of Man Sidecar TT in 1968 ridden by Terry Vinicombe.

often sponsored by BSA dealers, through to the late 1960s. Probably the final significant placing for a solo A65 was a third place in the 1968 750cc production TT by Tony Smith on a Spitfire with a race speed of 93.82mph (150.95km/h). But to place this in context, a 650 Triumph Bonneville won the event with the first 100mph (160km/h) lap of the TT circuit by a production machine. BSA's solo racing laurels were taken on by the Rocket 3.

During the early 1960s the American Motorcycle Association (AMA) was affiliated to the international motor racing controlling body, the FIM, and as a result the regulations controlling previously national events were changed to be more favourable to international entries. BSA decided to compete in the Daytona Races for 1966. The Daytona races were still subject to some AMA rules, which meant that there was a 500cc limit for ohv engines, but up to 750cc was

allowed for side valve engines. BSA decided to use the A50 as a basis for its racer, and four bikes were prepared by the factory. An additional two bikes were prepared in the USA.

The factory bikes were heavily modified and tuned, the most significant change being the replacement of the timing-side bush with a ball race, and the oil pump body being produced in cast iron to minimize distortion. Running a 10:1 compression ratio and twin 1³⁄₁₆ Amal GP carburettors, the Daytona bikes produced around 53bhp at 7,750rpm, with modified valve gear and special Hepworth and Grandage pistons allowing up to 8,250rpm in safety. Top speed was around 120mph (193km/h). Despite this promising performance, the actual race was a disaster when all six bikes retired.

BSA did not give up and continued to develop the bikes, entering the 1967 and 1968 races, but in both years failed to achieve any

ABOVE: The Daytona races of March 1967 proved unsuccessful for BSA. However the pride taken in the preparation of the A50 based racers is evident from this picture – note the use of a rear disk brake.

Pictured at the 1967 AM Daytona race, Robert Winters on #21 was one of the BSA team riders. He rode one of six A50-based racers in the 200-mile Expert race, all of which retired during the race.

ABOVE: Chris Vincent was the most successful BSA sidecar racer. Here he is in 1970 at the Cadwell International.

This close-up of Terry Vinicombe's Unit Twin powered outfit shows how suitable the engine was. Note the low height, twin GP carburettors and the coil ignition.

The Hanks brothers successfully campaigned BSA outfits in the 1960s and 1970s, with Norman Hanks winning the 1972 British Sidecar Championship. Here they are at Cadwell in 1969.

The BSA Unit Twins continue to be popular and competitive in classic racing. Here Pete Krukowski, who with passenger Chris McGahan dominated the scene in the 1980s, checks the timing on the Team 'Bon Accord' outfit.

significant success. However, the corporation's racing efforts were not totally in vain as Triumph also entered, using racing derivatives of its 500cc C-Series unit twins, and won in 1966 with Buddy Elmore riding and in 1967 with Gary Nixon riding. This is why Triumph called its sporting 500 twin the Daytona from 1967. The exercise also demonstrated that probably the best way to produce a competitive racer from a production model was to use a bored-out 500cc rather than a sleeved-down 650.

Sidecar Racing

Bert Perrigo in the 1962 article from the *Motor Cycle* was quoted as saying that the principal characteristic of the A65 was: 'The good, fat power curve, and that's something that the sidecar men in particular will be pleased about.' The proof of this statement was confirmed by the performance of the A65 in sidecar racing – possibly not quite what Bert Perrigo had in mind when making the quote!

Chris Vincent was a successful sidecar racer who worked for BSA in the 1960s. He started racing with the A7 and A10 series engine, but switched to the A65 unit in 1964. This was a unit derived from the Rocket motor, but sporting a twin carburettor head with dual Amal 1 5/32in GPs served by three float chambers to avoid fuel starvation problems, and a 10:1 compression ratio. The camshafts were production items from the US model and a close-ratio gearbox was used. Ignition was provided by the energy transfer system used on the Cyclone and Hornet models. The motor was estimated to make 60-

Despite the successes in the US flat-track racing, BSA still marketed the competition-biased Hornet to leisure-oriented customers. This is a 1967 model.

plus horsepower at 7,250rpm. Eventually, Vincent used three engines in his racers – 500 and 650cc fitted with five-speed gearboxes and a 750cc version with a four-speed box.

Probably Vincent's most famous victory was in 1965 at the Hutchinson 100 meeting at Silverstone, when he beat the Germans Scheidegger and Camathias on their BMW by a massive 45 seconds.

The example set by Chris Vincent lead to many other privateers using the A50 and A65 units in their racers. These included Peter Brown, Mick Boddice and Norman Hanks – and these racers dominated the UK sidecar racing scene from 1965 to well into the 1970s. Many notable victories were scored, including a 1–2–3 at the November 1967 Mallory Park meeting. This achievement was repeated in the 1968 IoM 750cc Sidecar TT when BSAs again took the first three places.

The most radical outfit powered by the unit twin was developed by Barry Kefford in 1971. His objective was to produce as low an outfit as possible, thus reducing drag. To achieve this, he cut the gearbox off of an A65, and laid the engine flat – creating a horizontal parallel twin. He used a separate Gold Star gearbox, and the chassis sported leading link forks and Austin Mini 12in wheels with disc brakes. However, by now the A65 engine was showing its age, so little lasting success was achieved. As an aside, there is an argument that it was no longer a unit engine so should not appear in this book!

In total, Chris Vincent won nine British sidecar road-racing championships on his unit-twin-powered outfit in 1964, 1965, 1969, 1970 and 1971, with the 1965 championship being won by Peter Brown and the 1972 by Norman Hanks. All in all, Bert Perrigo was right about the A65's ability to power a sidecar!

US Flat Track – The AMA Grand National

The A65 was used in the US for flat-track racing – this is where a group of riders compete around an oval dirt course, similar to a UK speedway track, but a mile or a half mile in total length. These races were run by the American Motorcycle Association (AMA) and in 1954 the yearly 'Grand National Championship' was set up. While the series was mainly flat-track events, a number of road races were incorporated to demonstrate a rider's versatility.

The flat-track format particularly favoured the twins, because of their slim profile and the torquey power delivery. BSA competed in these races, using unit twins from the mid 1960s, and often using proprietary frames made by independents such as Trackmaster. While some success was achieved by BSA riders such as Dick Mann, Jody Nicholas, Sammy Tanner, Ron Gould and Al Gunter in individual races, the Harley-Davidson riders held sway until the 1967 season, when Triumph rider Gary Nixon took the championship. So BSA was always up in the leader boards, but never won the championship nor took the Number 1 plate.

5 Owning and Riding Today

Introduction

In the early years of the new millennium, the A50 and A65 are still underrated motorcycles. The old rivals, Triumph's 500cc and 650cc unit twins, despite there being more of them available, still command a price premium over the compatible BSA products. However, this should be taken advantage of, for it means that the BSA twins are more affordable! With spares availability comparable to that of Triumph, adequate to good brakes, excellent frame, willing engines that can be made reliable, BSA unit twins make an intelligent choice for the classic enthusiast who wants a practical classic to ride and enjoy. That's as long as he or she is not too influenced by the charisma of the Triumph name. Of course, for those who want to put the cat among the pigeons, just mention to a die-hard Triumph fan that BSA bought Triumph way back in 1951!

This 1970 A65 Lightning is ripe for a cosmetic restoration. It is all there and largely standard, apart from the 1971-on handlebar switches.

The Issues

When running a classic bike today the owner needs to make the choice between originality and sensible modification that takes advantage of the body of knowledge and engineering solutions that have been learnt about the BSA model and classics in general. While the frame and suspension are largely satisfactory for day to day use, the main issues to be addressed with the A50 and A65 models can be broken down into a number of areas which comprise:

- engine
- primary drive
- ignition
- brakes
- electrics
- compression ratio/unleaded fuel/octane rating.

Each of these areas is explored in the following sections.

Engine Reliability Improvements

Of the tips given by Arthur (*see* box on page 125), the timing-side main bearing conversions, including the end feed of oil to the big ends, is a particularly useful modification to make as it gives a notionally stronger timing-side roller main bearing and positive location of the crank. It is also probably a good modification if the engine is expected to be ridden hard and far and will undoubtedly allow for longer periods between overhauls. It is probably a must if the engine capacity is being upped, and bearing in mind if performance is important, then big-bore kits are available to take the capacity up to 850cc.

As suggested elsewhere, the best oil pump for the unit twins is the 1971–72 cast iron version. These were, at the time of writing, very rare, but one should be fitted if available. At the very least, any oil pump should be reconditioned and the oil pressure release valve should also be checked and reconditioned.

Primary Drive and Gearbox

The clutch is generally pretty good when in good condition, but poor quality or worn friction plates and warped drive plates will cause dragging or slipping (or both!). The drive tabs on the plates also should be in good condition, and the corresponding slots in the basket and hub should not show wear. The most vital aspect of the clutch operation should be that the pressure plate is lifting squarely. If it is not, then all of the plates may not release properly, and the clutch will then heat up, causing swelling of the friction material and major drag and wear. Careful assembly and adjustment of a clutch with all its components in good condition (including a balanced set of springs) is the cure. The clutch springs (whether a four- or three-spring unit) should be tested by putting two together end to end, and pressing them together – usually in a vice. Both should compress the same amount – if one is 'softer' than the other it should compress first. If they do have different strengths, then replace the whole set. Various new improved clutch components are now being produced, including hard anodized alloy clutch baskets that are substantially lighter than the cast iron originals.

Devimead used to market an alloy clutch pressure plate which is more rigid than the pressed steel original and also incorporated a new thrust mechanism. In the standard set-up, the clutch pushrod bears against a hardened stud in the pressure plate, which was prone to wear. In the Devimead kit, the thrust mechanism comprised a set of needle rollers arranged radially on a carrier, which sat between a modified pushrod end with a flat bearing surface, and a new screw-in adaptor, again with a flat bearing surface. This provided a much increased pressure area, which made it more likely that the pressure plate was lifted squarely, and also as it was a much lower stressed mechanism it also benefited from reduced wear.

If the primary drive needs to be totally replaced, then a belt drive kit could be considered. The advantages are lightness (especially if alloy components are used), and smoothness. The general opinion is that belts seem to run smoother than a chain set-up.

The gearbox is reliable and has no generic weaknesses. If you are rebuilding the engine it is worthwhile to inspect all gearbox dogs for rounding or any other wear, the selector forks for wear and all teeth for damage. A final point, during maintenance you must not trust the early type of gearbox oil level indicator. This is a tube fixed to the gearbox drain plug, with its own drain plug concentric to the plug. When the inner plug is removed to check the level, some oil will always flow out. Do not take this as meaning the level is correct, as the tube will always collect some oil splash when the gearbox is in operation. If you rely on this as an indication of correct oil level, the gearbox will eventually run dry, as every time you check a little more oil is lost. The level indicator should be used only when topping up or refilling the gearbox, and a steady flow should be seen before replacing the plug.

There is room behind the engine, below the oil tank, to fit a Norton Commando type spin-off oil filter. It should increase engine life, and provide some additional oil capacity.

As an example of the sort of bike available during 2003, this 1970 Lightning is a good, honest example. Some surface rust and tarnishing is present but the original finish has held up well considering the bike was 34 years old when pictured.

Arthur's Tips

Arthur, of the bike shop 'Rockerbox' of Wrecclesham, is an experienced British bike mechanic, who has worked on the BSA unit twins as well as most of the other contemporary marques. When asked for some helpful hints and tips on working on the A65, his first response was 'trade it in for a good Triumph'. However, he did give the following as tips on the reassembly of the A50 and A65 engines.

● When setting up the crank end float, always assemble the drive-side main bearing on the crank with a shim – this gives you the space to pull the bearing off of the crank to adjust the shim width if needed. If you assemble it without a shim, then it is a lot harder to pull the main bearing inner race off the crank without damaging it. On final reassembly, use Loctite to fix the bearing firmly to the crank to help prevent it turning.
● If fitted, make sure you replace the sheet metal sprocket cover plate back in behind the gearbox sprocket first before putting the engine in – because you won't get it back in with the engine in the frame!
● Make sure that the spilt pin is present in the rocker oil feed in the head – this has two functions. Firstly, it restricts flow to the appropriate level, preventing excessive volumes of oil flooding the rocker box, and possibly being drawn down the guides and causing smoking. Secondly, it helps to keep the oil way clear of sludge, which may block it resulting in the valve gear being starved of oil.
● Fit a full flow oil filter in the oil return line. This modification is cheap and easy and will protect the engine and especially the vulnerable timing-side main bush. A further benefit is that it will increase oil capacity, which on the oil-in-frame models is considered to be marginal by some.
● Fit an oil cooler, especially to oil-in-frame models, as these do run hot. As with the oil filter, this will also give a useful increase in oil capacity.

Ignition System

As described above, the initial A50s and A65s were equipped with Lucas 4CA contact breaker points – these do not allow for individual timing of both cylinders apart from by altering the points gap and are hence difficult and fiddly to set up accurately. The 4CA back plate was superseded for 1968 by the Lucas 6CA contact breaker assembly and back plate, and it is worthwhile upgrading to this contact breaker set-up if a bike still has the 4CA contact breakers. Do not forget to keep the contact breaker cam felt 'wick' when fitted lightly oiled to minimize wear on the contact breaker heel. The auto advance unit should be checked regularly and lubricated sparingly but often. The springs in particular can stretch or lose their tension, giving over-advanced ignition, which can cause major engine problems. A change in the exhaust note – going 'flatter' – can be an indication of problems in this area.

Electronic ignition is probably the main innovation that has transformed old British bikes. At a stroke, the rigmarole of setting and maintaining the timing, and the consequent performance and starting problems can be eliminated. Unreliable advance/retard units and fast-wearing contact breaker points can be thrown away and replaced with electronic units with no moving or wearing parts. Accurate timing is maintained at all times and starting is usually easier. There are two downsides – if the ignition system fails it is hard to fix on the side of the road and the most popular systems rely on a good healthy battery. However, the failure rate of these systems appears to be very low, and with the improved battery, charging and regulating technology available today this should not be a problem. Certainly, the risk of something failing in a well-maintained, modern electronic system is a lot lower than that of relying on a set of mechanical contact breaker points and a mechanical advance/retard unit that could be forty years old. The only downside of fitting one of the proprietary electronic ignition systems, such as Boyer Bransden, is that there is no independent adjustment of the timing on individual cylinders, just like the original 4CA contact breakers. However, this does not seem to be an issue – perhaps because the units are accurately

In 1972 Devimead offered the A70 750cc engine in their own running gear. This shot was taken at the annual Racing and Sporting Show held at London's Horticultural Halls in the 1970s.

manufactured and do not need to provide the adjustment in the first place.

Belt conversion kits are available for the primary drive, providing smoother running and seeming to cut down on vibration. The original four-spring BSA clutch can be replaced with the equivalent Triumph 650 article, which can ease sourcing of clutch plates and springs. Alloy clutch baskets are also available, which offer significant weight savings. The gearbox is reliable and no aftermarket parts appear to be generally available, probably an indication of lack of demand.

Braking

In general, the brakes provided throughout the lifetime and range of the A50 and A65 models were adequate to good – with the exception of the original A50 7in unit. The application of

common sense and good maintenance is probably the most important factor regarding the brakes, using them to ensure that the brakes as provided are working at their full efficiency. To achieve this, there are a number of points that must be addressed.

Firstly, make sure that the cables are in good condition, with no frayed wires or loose (or, even worse, solderless) nipples. Make sure that in all cables the inner moves freely within the outer, and, where required, the cables are well lubricated using the correct lubricant for the type of cable fitted. Note that some modern cables should not be lubricated or require specific treatments – check with the supplier of the cable. One problem that I have found with a number of cables bought recently is excess solder left on the nipple. Cable end nipples should be free to revolve a few degrees in the handlebar levers; if they are a tight fit or stiff then this will have a major effect on the brake as it will increase the effort needed to put on the brake. Test them by releasing the cable from the adjuster and seeing if the cable pivots freely around the nipple at the handlebar lever end. If the cable does not turn, then the likely cause is excessive solder on the nipple that fouls the lever recess. Ease off any excess solder on the nipple with a fine file, and put a drop of oil on the nipple. At the other end, clevis pins connecting the cable to the brake arm should be loose enough to allow the cable to revolve around them – again, if they are stiff then ease the hole in the fitting on the end of the cable a bit and lubricate sparingly. Make sure that the clevis pin is tight but also able to revolve in the hole in the brake arm. If it does not fit freely or is too loose, then replace it.

The brake levers on the front and rear drums should have an angle of less than 90 degrees to the cable. If the angle is greater than 90 degrees then the brake will still work, but will need more force applied to get the same braking effect. If the angle is greater than 90 degrees, then there is something wrong in the set-up of the brake – either the arm is not fitted on to the correct spline or there is excessive wear in the brake. Find out which it is and fix it. Brake shoes must be in good condition – the workshop manual should give wear tolerances. Shoes will wear to fit a hub, so if you fit new shoes braking performance may be poor to begin with. Old brake shoes will be likely to contain asbestos, and suitable pre-cautions must be taken when working on them. If you are in any doubt as to what precautions should be taken, seek professional advice from a suitably qualified person or organization.

Upgrades to standard brakes can be carried out fairly easily, and can be done using parts from later models. For example, early A50s would benefit from having an A65 8in brake fitted, and all 500cc and 650cc early models would benefit from fitting the 8in Triumph type TLS brake. The fitting of later brakes may require modifying or changing the fork legs to those of the appropriate later model. The oil-in-frame models with the conical front brake can be improved by careful adjustment and setting up, or the whole front end can be replaced with a disc front end from an oil-in-frame Triumph. Note that the Triumph disc front wheels are wider than the conical hub type. If this route is taken, then new yokes are required as well as wheel, fork legs and the associated disc caliper, master cylinder and hydraulic plumbing.

Electrical Improvements

Unless the originality of the bike is more important than peace of mind when riding, the 6V electrical system should be upgraded to 12V. Advantages include lower power loss through reduced resistance (which is a definite advantage with old and corroded connections), potentially giving much brighter lights front and rear, and easier sourcing of bulbs (the bikes still vibrate and can get through a lot of bulbs!). A 12V conversion also enables the fitting of a modern headlight unit (such as the Wipac Quadoptic), which uses the modern car type halogen bulbs available in most garages – it can be hard to find the earlier types of bulbs, even in 12V versions outside of specialist stockists, and you will always need one at 7:00pm as you prepare to ride to a club night! Upgrades are relatively easy to

With no moving parts, the Boyer electronic ignition is a fit-and-forget system.

achieve, but should be done properly and carefully. You can even retain the original Lucas light and ignition switches fitted to the head-lamp on the earlier bikes, but if so make sure the plugs that fit into the switch units are properly fixed in. A cable tie can be looped around the plug and switch to ensure that the plugs are secure, as total ignition or light failure will result if they do fall off – which you can guarantee that they will at the most inopportune time!

On early 6V bikes (up to the 1965 model year) the battery carrier is relatively small, and is fixed to the frame using two bolts in its base, under the rubber mat. Later models from 1966 had a new carrier, which had its top rubber mounted to lugs welded on to the frame. This carrier is of a generous size, and can take a standard 12V battery. The early carrier (easily recognized as it has two fixing bolts on the bottom of the tray that bolt on to the frame) will not take the standard size British 12V battery, as it measures only 12.5cm (width), 6cm (depth) and 13cm (height). However, a rummage through your friendly local dealer should turn up a suitable 12V battery – for example a Rob

Hunter YB5L-B (RHB 39) is a 12V, 5-amp/hour battery that fits with no modifica-tions. Even if you are running electronic ignition, capacity should be adequate, and it meets the original battery specification, although most modern 12V batteries now are 7- or 9-amp hour capacity.

If the alternator stator does not have its coils encapsulated in resin then it is probably over thirty-five years old, and the insulation will be breaking down. Even if it appears to be serviceable when tested, once it heats up in the hot and oily environment of the primary chaincase it will very probably be breaking down and producing less power than it should. It is better to avoid problems and replace it with a modern unit. The rotor may be all right. As described in Chapter 7, the rule of thumb test is to see if the magnets can support the rotor when picked up with a spanner – if all of them can, then the magnets should be up to strength. The second thing to look at is that the rotor centre is not breaking up. If the rotor passes these tests, then there should be no problem in reusing it.

With a 12V system, the voltage regulation can

The angle between the brake arm and the cable must be less than 90 degrees for maximum efficiency.

be improved using off the shelf components – on the 6V system the best option is to change to 12V. The main objective is to move away from the switched system using solid state electronics to regulate the alternator output. The original equipment 12V system rectifier and zener diode both work well. Early 12V systems will benefit from having the zener diode relocated from its position under the seat to the later position under the bottom yoke with a decent heat sink in the fresh air. Replacement of the original plate type rectifiers can be achieved at very low cost using one of the square solid state rectifiers, although you will need to make sure that you run an earth lead to the unit.

The charging, rectification and regulation aspects can also be upgraded using one of the solid state combined rectifiers and charge control modules (or black box) currently on the market. These will be an attractive option to those converting to 12V or to renovators with missing parts as the total cost is very close to that of an individual zener, rectifier and heat sink. They should also be more efficient than both the original plate type and the replacement solid state rectifiers, leading to less power loss in the overall system.

Retrofitting indicators is a good idea with modern traffic conditions, and can be easily done using components that are not out of keeping with the age of the machine – for example, using pattern Lucas type indicators, which are readily available at auto jumbles. If done carefully, there is no need either to drill holes in metalwork or to alter an original loom, meaning that the indicators can be removed later if originality is important.

The BSA loom was good quality, and was typical of the period, using mainly bullet connectors for wire to wire joins, and spade types to connect to switches and other components. The loom was wrapped in cloth sleeving, which provided both a protective function in resisting rubbing, and helped to tidy up the loom. Most problems, if the loom has not been bodged, can be put down to wires fracturing, dodgy or dirty connectors, and worn insulation. The cloth outer

covering will probably be showing signs of age as well, with holes worn in it and general fraying, although often the state of the outer makes the loom look worse than it is. The wire and insulation will harden with age and be more prone to breakage from wear and vibration. Old wiring looms do deteriorate, and as the subjects could be over forty years old, replacement is a lot easier than thorough refurbishment. If originality is vital, then it is possible to replace the wires in the harness and reuse the original cloth outer casing. This is only worth doing if the outer is worth saving.

Connectors will corrode and wear, giving rise to intermittent faults and higher electrical resistance, reducing performance of all components, such as the lights. Note that each connection has two points of failure if wires are not soldered – these are at the wire to the fitting (spade or bullet), and at the fitting to the component or other fitting. Insulation will be worn through in tight spots, giving intermittent short circuits. If the loom is in apparently good condition, then it is worthwhile to check for continuity of each wire in the loom; check the resistance of each wire in the loom and take apart and clean and lubricate all of, the connectors and switches. Reassemble them with some form of lubricant such as Vaseline to protect them. If you replace some of, or the entire loom, or any connectors, it is worthwhile to crimp then solder any new connectors rather than use crimping alone. New standard looms are available, or, if you are modifying the electrics to take advantage of the modern electronic ignition and charging units, a custom-made loom is reasonably easy to produce. After all, you have the bike itself to use as a jig!

Compression Ratio/Unleaded Fuel/Octane Rating

Finally, there is one last aspect to running a classic bike in the UK – the availability of suitable fuel. Currently there is only unleaded fuel widely available in the UK, and very limited supplies of leaded petrol (usually 95 Octane) available through a few outlets. The introduction of unleaded fuel in the UK was caused by the health issues associated with lead, but has raised two major issues: the first is valve seat recession; the second is the octane rating.

Valve seat recession is caused by the valve hammering at its seat, which results in the valve wearing away the seat and thus moving up into the seat. With leaded fuel, a thin layer of lead was deposited on the set, giving a cushioning effect. With unleaded petrol, there are no additives that perform this function, so the valve hits the seat with no cushion, causing wear to the seat. Should valve seat recession occur, the main symptom is the valve clearances closing up. Ultimately, the valve could be held open on the tappet, causing both blow-by and even faster erosion of the seat and possibly damage to the camshaft and followers.

The advent of unleaded petrol caused a great deal of speculation in the press as to its effect on classic bikes and cars. The ultimate solution is to replace the valve seats with suitably hardened ones, using modern materials that are designed to run in an unleaded environment. However, it is still unclear if this is an issue with a classic bike doing a few thousand miles a year. If the bike has been run on leaded petrol in the past there will still be some lead on the seats, so with low

mileage this residual lead may remain for some years. There is also a wide range of lead replacement additives available for adding to petrol, although there is no clear evidence regarding their effectiveness.

The second problem with unleaded petrol is the octane rating. Standard unleaded is usually rated as 92 Octane, which is not as high an octane as UK 'four-star' was, and hence can cause pinking in a high-compression engine. The solutions are: to use super-unleaded, which is 95 Octane; to reduce the timing advance; or to use an octane booster – or any combination of these.

At the end of the day, it is the owner's choice – some people have run bikes on unleaded with no detrimental effects, while others have suffered. I personally have had experience of running a 1970 Triumph Bonneville on super-unleaded, doing around 1,000 miles per year with no damage. It will pink on ordinary unleaded, but not on super-unleaded, which is of the higher octane. The valves were reground on assembly, which would have removed any lead residue, but I have detected no abnormal valve wear after several years' running. Admittedly, this has not involved either high mileage or particularly hard riding, so my experience may not be applicable to all.

6 Twin True Stories

Introduction

This chapter has been created with the assistance of previous and current owners of A65s. It aims to provide an owner's view of what the bike was and is like to own and ride today, looking at ease of ownership, problems, high and low spots and any other anecdotes that are interesting.

1962 A65 Star

Jeremy Scott bought his late-1962 model year A65 Star in 1969, when it was six years old.

He had had an unfortunate experience with a BSA Spitfire Special Mk II, which was a 'bag of nails' and had been nothing but trouble, and so was looking for a reliable 650 to use for day to

Rockers used the A65 in the 1960s! This period shot is from 1964 and shows the scene outside Squires Café – prominent is the 1963 Rocket with period modifications of clip-ons and the leopard skin pattern seat cover.

Jeremy's 1962 shows some modifications and many standard features. TLS front brake, seat and mudguards are obvious modifications.

The drive side reveals the early chaincase with its oval cover for the clutch adjuster holes, and the non-standard silencers.

day commuting between his digs and university in Birmingham, and for longer trips, either to return home to Bishop's Stortford, Hertfordshire, and to visit his girlfriend of the time in Bridgwater, Somerset. Jeremy bought the bike from an old grey-haired scrap dealer based near Epping Forest, at a place called Woodford Common, on the old A11. There the scrap dealer had a series of connected corrugated iron sheds, in which he had literally thousands of old British bikes that were being slowly broken up for spares. The dealer said that he had a bike that he had known from new, an early A65 with 28,000 miles on the clock. It was hitched up to a sports sidecar, so was on sidecar gearing. The bike appeared to be all original, but was coloured in BSA Metallic Gold. This may indicate that it was a special order from the factory, or had been resprayed at some time, as the standard colours for 1962 were Sapphire Blue, Flamboyant Red or Black. The scrap dealer said he thought that this would be a reliable bike – Jeremy bought it not based on this 'guarantee', but because he liked the bike and in the event the dealer's words were proved to be true. The scrap dealer's son literally hacksawed off the sidecar, and Jeremy rode it away for £25.

The gear lever shaft is spindly and caused some problems. The spindle is practically half the width of the equivalent Triumph item.

Jeremy then rode the bike until he could not stand the Gold colour any more, and during 1969–70, he stripped the bike down and resprayed it in the Metallic Red that it still bears today – albeit a bit faded.

In 1971 he carried further cosmetic work by replacing the original mudguards with proprietary alloy ones, as the originals were in poor condition, and repainting the frame using 'Brushing Belco' black cellulose. He also took the opportunity to replace the original 18in front wheel with SLS 8in brake with a BSA/Triumph 1968 19in wheel with the corporate TLS brake. This wheel actually was attached to an A10 when it came into Jeremy's possession! Jeremy found the original brake to be very poor, to quote: 'The brake it came with was so poor that it was a bit like whistling as the lorry approached!' The corporate TLS brake was found to be a great improvement.

For security, he replaced the standard ignition lock, which could be operated with a screwdriver, with a car type ignition switch with a proper key, which he mounted in the nacelle, and, being at university in Birmingham, managed to get a new key for the steering lock from Len Vale Onslow's emporium. Jeremy then rode the bike regularly in that condition for the next six to seven years.

Over the years of riding, when the bike was his only form of transport, Jeremy had very few

The later 1968 TLS brake was fitted to cope with 1970s traffic. Note the original Y type bracket supporting the non-standard alloy mudguard on the fork legs.

problems. In his own words: 'It always dripped oil – but they all did that sir!' Other faults were few and far between, or trivial. The bike virtually always had a dodgy gear change return spring, causing the gear change lever to flop about – but this didn't affect the operation to any great extent so was lived with. The splines on the gear lever shaft were weak:

C15-like spline gives up on the gear lever, so you have to employ various means to try to tighten up the gap between the level and the shaft, and eventually you have to replace the shaft inside, which I did once. Once you got the level tightened up it was fine, but it was such a fine spline that it would let go easily – a bit of a flimsy beast.

The nacelle gave Jeremy some moments when the headlamp fell out due to the adjuster ring behind the chrome surround coming loose. Note also the original chronometric speedometer, additional car type ignition switch and sensible position of the steering lock on the top of the forks.

The majority of issues that Jeremy had were electrical. It was and still is a 6V system. There was a constant need to keep the contact breakers set correctly and the condensers needed to be replaced on a regular basis. The coils never gave any trouble, and have never been replaced. Jeremy believes that they are the originals as supplied with the bike. The old selenium plate rectifier was replaced with a silicon one. Alternators gave him a lot of problems – the coils on the original alternators (the ones with the non-potted coils) used to loosen off and then connections would break. An example of a typical alternator problem was experienced when driving down to his workplace in Somerset down the M5: 'Driving down to Somerset on time and lo and behold the lights suddenly went blindingly bright, and the bike started to make some 'orrible clunky noises, and I thought that I was going to loose the bottom end because I could feel the vibration coming out of the drive side.'

Jeremy continued to ride down the M5, hoping to get up that long hill that climbs up into the Mendips, and succeeded, so then rode downhill towards Bridgwater. By now, he was off the motorway, and eventually got to about five miles from his destination when the engine stopped with a big clonk. It was seized solid, and would not turn over even when it had cooled off. He pushed the bike into work, and then the following weekend set about fixing the problem. He did have some concerns as to where he was going to get spares from in the depths of darkest Somerset! Expecting to find major bottom-end problems, and possibly seized pistons, he started by dismantling the top end. He was amazed to find that, when he pulled off the barrels, the pistons flopped forwards and the big ends appeared to be fine. This was a bit puzzling, as he was expecting the big ends to have suffered oil starvation if the mains had seized. So, still convinced the main bearing must be gone, he decided to lighten the engine before pulling it out of the frame, by dismantling the primary drive. On pulling off the primary drive case, various nuts that should have been attached to something fell out, the alternator stator was 'squiffy' on its studs, the rotor nut was undone and had cut a nice round groove in the inside of the chaincase. He tapped the stator straight, and the motor was magically un-seized. The mains seemed to be fine, so Jeremy put the engine back together and started the bike up. The engine was fine, the clonking had gone and even the alternator still worked and was charging the battery.

The other endearing habit that the bike had was that the nacelle ring, which held the headlamp on and allowed for adjustment, would fall off from time to time – usually in the dark. He never lost the thing completely, but did have some moments as the headlamp flew around connected to the bike only by its wires!

Vibration only reared its head at about an estimated 80mph – the speed being the approximate middle of the speedometer's reading as it vibrated from side to side through a 60-degree arc at that speed.

The engine was rebuilt in 1978, and to Jeremy's surprise the crank was still within the original manufacturing tolerances – both on the big ends and the timing-side journal. He put this down to the regular oil changes, which he carried out at intervals of less than 2,000 miles. In 1983–84 the frame paint was touched up again, and the wheels were rebuilt with new rims, but he did not use the bike much after that.

The bike has never really let him down apart from the tale recounted above – and Jeremy sees no reason to get rid of it. He feels a bond to the bike, and still likes its looks and the way it behaves on the road.

1972 A65 Firebird Scrambler

Chris Burrell has owned his oil-in-frame model A65 Firebird Scrambler since 1993, and has ridden it sparingly since then. It was manufactured in August 1971 and therefore was one of the first of the 1972 model year. As such, it represents the last of the line of the A65 series, the BSA oil-in-frame line and BSA itself.

The bike was reimported back from the USA and as far as Chris knows has never had any major engine work or been restored before he bought it – one of the reasons that he bought the bike was because of its original and untouched condition. The current mileage was just over 5,000, and there were numerous indications of the bike's originality. These included the original brown-coloured speedometer and tachometer cables, and the fact that the frame retained the original features, such as the US-market regulations conformance sticker on the headstock.

The only obvious deviation from standard is the lack of the red pin striping on the small capacity export petrol tank, between the Etruscan Bronze top panel and the White lower panel on the tank. The frame was in its original Black enamel – BSA moved away from the Dove Grey (read dirty white) frame colour for the 1972 season, and the front brake plate was also in a black finish – again correct for the 1972 year.

The headstock of Chris's Firebird still carries the manufacturer's standards sticker as required by the US authorities.

The timing side looks almost bare without the pipes. The rear conical hub and abbreviated mudguard are obvious.

From the drive side the high-level exhaust system and full-sized silencers dominate the styling.

As it stands, the bike is in very good original condition and is pretty much completely standard mechanically and cosmetically. It bears some slight knocks and scratches as should be expected of a bike which is more than three decades old, but the original finish has stood up very well to the test of time, reflecting well on the standards that BSA was still applying to its bikes even at the very end of the company's existence. Chris has not fitted an after-market oil filter, instead relying on regular oil changes every 1,000 to 2,000 miles. He also does not believe in electronic ignition, as he doesn't mind the 'spannering' and prefers to have the option to be able to carry out roadside repairs rather than being stranded should an electronic ignition system fail.

Interestingly, the bike even retained its original contact breaker points. Chris has found no problems with the standard contact breaker points set-up, and this was demonstrated by the easy starting of the bike after it had been standing for some months. Mechanically, the bike was excellent. The bike burst into life after a couple of kicks, sounding mechanically quiet and only displaying a slight degree of temperament due to the pilot jet in one carburettor being gummed up with old petrol – even this cleared up after a couple of minutes. Once that glitch had cleared, it ran very quietly and smoothly. Chris has had no electrical or mechanical problems at all, and this bike demonstrates that even at the end of the production run, BSA was still capable of producing the reliable, well finished bikes that they were renowned for during the preceding decades.

The exhaust pipes and silencers are of special interest – they were finished in Black Chrome as

The black-chromed pipes are well preserved. The bike retains its sump guard and folding footrests.

standard, not black heat-resistant paint. Cannings, the plating firm, put in a special set of equipment to enable Small Heath to achieve the superior finish and corrosion resistance that the black chroming process could achieve – which was especially important for the exhaust system, as it formed a significant contribution to the overall appearance of the bike. Again, in line with the overall finish of the bike the pipes were in excellent condition and showed no obvious signs of their age.

Chris admits that he has not used the bike a lot – he bought it because it is one of his favourites and he takes pleasure in owning it. However, the engine is quiet – a lot quieter than the equivalent Triumph 'bag of nails', and the riding position is great. The handlebars, of the original high and wide US specification, mean a comfortable and pleasant riding position, although the rubber mounting does give some 'looseness' and takes a bit of getting used to. Chris has not had any

problems from vibration from the bike – he has never experienced 'white knuckle' syndrome despite some long trips, and reckons that if vibration does appear it is down to something loosening off. A quick spanner check before use is recommended.

Handling and road holding Chris finds, and I quote, 'lovely' – the bike can be laid over very nicely. Chris reckoned that although the bike is heavy, it didn't feel heavy – even at 2mph it was very easy to handle and felt sturdy and stable, and these traits were maintained up to decent road speeds. We agreed that this indicated that the frame was probably designed with the A65 unit in mind rather than the Triumph engine (further proof of this theory is the problems that Meriden had in fitting the Triumph engine into the frame at the start of production. The engine could not be fitted without taking off the rocker boxes, which then could not be refitted to the

Despite being only 6in in diameter, Chris finds the lights are good. The Thunderbolt and Lightning both had 7in headlamps.

engine in frame, necessitating the redesign of the rocker boxes to make them fit).

The front brake Chris described as 'brilliant'. This may surprise readers who have read the bad press that the brake has received, but Chris reckoned that his brake could lock up the front wheel at any speed – and admitted to being caught out by it on occasion. He put the performance down to the fact that the brake was set up correctly and had not been messed about with. The old myth of the alloy hub expanding faster than the shoes was dismissed with the shrewd observation that the hub had a steel liner forming the braking surface and that some critics obviously did not know what they were talking about. He went on to say that he has often seen conical front brakes in tests that are obviously wrongly set up, with the operating levers at all angles, which does affect their performance. But with the brake correctly set up and not 'messed with' – and with decent shoes – he has had no problems. The rear brake, however, Chris reckoned was weak and could fade.

The lights were excellent, even with the smaller 6-inch headlamp. The 1971 Firebirds had by then moved the dip switch to the handlebars, making night riding a lot safer. All the electrics still worked and the inclusion of the capacitor in the ignition circuit was singled out by Chris as one of the major steps forward made by Lucas, as it removed the need for a charged battery to be present – even if the battery was flat the bike could still be started with a couple of kicks.

Riding the bike, Chris felt that it could easily keep up with modern A-road traffic and the best bit was the reaction of so many people to seeing the bike on the road. Everyone liked the bike – its noise and appearance. Chris felt that it has that 'something' or 'X factor' that makes him just love the bike – the thing that the marketing staff of any company wish they could identify!

1972 Model BSA A65 Lightning

Keeping with the later bike theme that runs through this chapter, the author's brother, Nick, bought a 1972 model A65 Lightning in 1976 between leaving school and going to university. The bike cost £550, and was actually manufactured in October 1971, but first registered in 1973 with an 'M' suffix – step forward SWL 877M, engine and frame number A65L NG002255.

This was, in Nick's own words, his 'first real bike', and was one of the last A65s to be registered. Previously, Nick had owned a 1970 B175 Bantam, which was part-exchanged for the A65 – I believe the dealer said that he would give the trade-in price only if Nick rode the Bantam into the dealership for the exchange. This could be somewhat challenging as the dealership was some 20 miles from home – and the reliability of the Bantam was so suspect that a 20-mile trip was problematic to say the least. But the dealership was close to where Nick worked, and the foreman owed Nick a favour so the works van was pressed into service to transport the Bantam just close enough to the dealer's premises to appear to have 'done the distance', and the deal was struck.

Appearance-wise, Nick thought that the bike had the nicest lines of the entire BSA unit twin range – though this may well be a controversial view, bearing in mind that his bike had the large UK-specification fuel tank (also known as the 'breadbin') and possibly the greenest custom paint job I have ever seen. This comprised a sort of fish-scale pattern over the tank and side panels, in a light green with white highlights – an unusual looking paint job, but, to give its due, it was very well executed with a deep shine and depth that put the original paint job to shame. The other British bike owners at university christened the bike 'The Bathroom Suite'. Luckily, only black and white photos of the bike survive . . . The paint job was fortunately combined with the later Black enamelled frame and standard chrome mudguards, giving a restrained contrast to the extravagance!

This is Nick on his 1972 Lightning back in 1977. Think yourself lucky that the picture is in black and white, as the bright green paintwork was truly startling!

The bike came with a standard low-level exhaust system with the corporate megaphone silencers – which I still think are some of the best silencers British industry produced, being not too loud, but looking great! (As an aside, when I tried to buy a set for a T140E I owned in the mid 1980s, Darrel at 'Rockerbox' refused to sell me them, claiming that they were very prone to vibration splitting – which was true, but they looked so much better than the alternatives!)

Nick is not a slow rider, and enjoyed (and still enjoys) riding his bikes to the full. He especially liked the acceleration that the A65 provided, and the first of many blow-ups occurred about six months after purchase. In his own words:

In traffic on the way into work I trickled to the front of the queue at the lights where three lanes were about to reduce to two. A truck and a bus on my left, a car to the right, I sit there in first with the clutch in, the lights change, I drop the clutch . . . and the engine bogs as the bike staggers forward; blast, that must have been second. Slip clutch and give it more revs, engine howls, bike reluctantly moves forwards some more, car and bus now converging on me fast, I pull in the clutch, stamp right foot down and engage first with right foot, drop clutch, bike jumps forward like a goosed kangaroo and I lose my grip on the left-hand bar. Make no mistake, for a 650 the A65 had a surprising turn of speed – a year or so later I gave a friend on a then new Kawasaki Z900 a standing-start drag (Double Overhead Camshaft it said – dead impressive), and up to 65 the BSA was the quicker. Today, though, I really wanted it to slow down, but unfortunately I couldn't release the throttle until I got a grip with my other hand. This I did in probably less than a second, all the time watching the tachometer go through 6, 7, 8,000rpm (power started to drop off here), to just before 9,000rpm when a loud and expensive-sounding bang coincided with the power virtually vanishing and my regaining control of the handlebars. By now, I was 200yd clear of the other traffic, which promptly came past me. But she was still running, albeit trailing a plume of smoke, so we limped the 10 miles or so into work, bike sounding like a cement mixer, where, in the car park, she stopped dead and wouldn't even turn over on the kick-start.

The author was entrusted with rebuilding the bike, and, surprise, surprise, the standard A65 problems had occurred. The drive-side big end had gone, comprehensively enough to allow the piston to touch the flywheel – but luckily not causing enough damage to need replacement of either. The timing-side bush was of course also

worn. Regrinds were needed on the big ends and the timing-side bush, a new undersized bush to suit was fitted and the engine was rebuilt. Nick, who had in the meantime gone up to university in North Wales, had to come back down to Hampshire in January to ride the 200 miles back to university through a snowstorm. He practically had to be lifted off the bike when he arrived, and counts this as one of his more memorable rides – but not necessarily for the right reasons!

While at university, the A65 was Nick's only form of transport and he drove her virtually every day. Then, of course, the troubles really started for this BSA. Student grants weren't too generous and offers of cheap beer were, so maintenance as far as the BSA was concerned was limited to buying petrol and bolting back on the bits that Nick noticed coming loose – this included the carburettors, for example, and foot pegs and indicators. And rear brake levers. And

The final year oil-in-frame models had conventional black frames and the large 4 gallon fuel tank. This example was for sale at Kempton Park Autojumble in January 2004.

tachometer drives. And pannier mounts. And handlebars . . . in retrospect, Nick realized that it would have been cheaper in the long run if he'd spent a little time with spanners tightening some of the bits he didn't notice falling off. Like, for example, the 'anti-drum bar' under the tank. He spotted this had fallen off, but:

> My practised mechanic's eye told me that the bar clearly didn't hold the tank on, so had obviously only been put there as a bit of BSA frippery. So I didn't bother to replace it, and smugly congratulated myself on improving the power-to-weight ratio. A few weeks later I started to notice an occasional distinct smell of petrol when I braked. The penny finally dropped just after I'd filled the tank and stopped at some lights – a huge smell of petrol and a load of steam from the front of the bike. Closer examination revealed the steam to be petrol vapour, caused by neat four star cascading from the split across the front of the tank. Fixing this with Araldite was the first of many maintenance escapades that sort of worked in the short term but were clearly, even without the benefit of hindsight, doomed to failure.

So the 'Curse of the A65 Vibration' had struck – but, to be fair to the bike, the 'anti-drum bar', as Nick described it, was actually there to stop the tank flexing and opening up the seams that held the two sides of the tank together. . .

Next problem that arose was unusual on A65s – it was the gearbox. The dogs on second gear rounded, so the bike would just jump out of gear. Nick rightly put this down to his fondness for second gear – and using all the revs available, which meant ignoring the notional 6,400 redline: 'Hey – I knew power was good up to 8,000rpm. She'd pull gloriously from around 35 to 70mph, making second my favourite around-town gear. I solved that problem by ignoring second for a year, holding first to about 40 or so, then dropping into third.'

This, of course, led to further problems. For the latter half of that year, Nick's bike had dreadful clutch problems – no matter what he did to adjust it, give it 30 miles and it started slipping, give it another 20 and it started

dragging as well. Changing the plates helped a little, but it wasn't until about the fifth time that he was sitting on the street looking at the dismantled clutch yet again that he realized the basket had broken. Nick was wondering why the basket didn't actually run on the bearings:

> There was a bearing plate that the basket was just seated on, and not particularly well, but by now I was used to BSA's sloppy tolerances. Then, as I looked and tried to match the components against the oil-stained drawings in my trusty Haynes manual, I suddenly realized that the basket had broken – the middle of it had fractured all around the bearing housing and what I assumed to be a bearing plate was actually the centre of the basket, edges worn smooth by miles of riding it like that. One basket later and the clutch worked properly.

All these high revs had obviously been taking their toll:

> When the front mudguard brackets fractured I tried a similar pragmatic approach by removing them – after all, Captain America in *Easy Rider* didn't need a mudguard, did he? Well, no, but then he also didn't have to drive every day in North Wales. Unusually, once I'd taken the broken mudguard off, it didn't rain for over a week . . . and then it did. Driving ten miles in an open-face helmet without a front mudguard in the rain is not something I'd recommend. It's not the water that gets you (after all, you get that from rain). No, it's the dirty water. Riding along I could see a brackish plume rising in front of me then apparently arcing back to take me in the face, eyes, nose, mouth . . . it took a week's brushing to make my teeth feel clean again. So that meant a cheap alloy guard from a breaker's yard. It wasn't until I tried mounting it that it became clear it was for an 18in wheel, but hacksawing the back off it soon stopped it rubbing against the tyre.

So, all in all, it was an eventful year of riding. Nick was beginning to realize that some maintenance was needed, especially as by this time the exhaust system was also suffering from vibration-induced fractures so:

Next summer I got it home and treated it to a bit of love and affection, ahem, Siamese pipes, reverse cone megaphone and new second-hand gearbox. All quick and easy to fit, pipe-reduced weight and, most importantly, all cheap. Also fitted a smaller gearbox sprocket for more acceleration (stupidly big job, this, as you've got to go through the gearbox or split the crankcases to get at it). There was a tad of a misfire, too, at high revs, so I fitted new condensers. I also fitted a new zener diode, stopping the battery boiling, and a new throttle cable. The single cable from the twistgrip broke, so to get home I tied the inner to my belt and tried to control revs with my body position. This didn't work too well at first, as it was hard to stop accelerating; judicious use of the kill switch got that problem under some sort of control and I got home in one piece, but put a new cable at the top of my parts to get list.

All sorted, I rode her back up to Wales in September. And as I got on the M4 I realized it wasn't all sorted at all – that misfire was still there and getting worse. By the time I reached Swindon it was getting bad at 3,500rpm, so the rest of the journey was spent at as close to 3,500 as I could manage. It took a long time. Back at the digs I replaced the condensers – still no luck. Carbs seemed fine, so reluctantly I decided to whip the head off, once again in the open air. All seemed fine as I examined the head, and then had a peak at the piston crowns. Each inlet valve cut-away had a neat half moon apparently cast into it . . . oh dear. Yup, the springs had given up the unequal struggle against constant over-revving, and in retrospect I think I was pretty lucky not to drop a valve. Both were noticeably bent, both were replaced, new pistons were sourced and the misfire finally vanished for good.

So, what was she like to ride? Nick found her surprisingly good, actually. She was:

About as fast as a 750 Bonneville and handled as well (which meant a lot better than the contemporary Japanese bikes – Honda CX500s, Suzuki Hustlers, CB200s etc.). I remember one bike club run where they took about half a dozen bikes (mine the only Brit) to the top of the Llanberis pass, stopped for a cup of tea, then came down the south side. Lovely twisty road, lots of open corners and reasonably steep. So I set off last, kicked the BSA into neutral and switched her off, and coasted down the mountain hands off, steering with body weight, slowing with rear brake and passing all the other Jap bikes on my way. Most enjoyable, though it didn't really make up for the overall lack of reliable power – strictly speaking, she was no faster than a typical Japanese 250, and you could guarantee that if you tried to keep up with one for more than about 10 miles something on the BSA would break or drop off. Vibration over 4,000rpm was really quite fearsome.

Many of the problems identified were down to the vibration. So the handling was good, if not the overall performance in comparison with other bikes. So what about the brakes? Again, in Nick's own words:

One benefit, though, of an overall lack of reliable power, was that the brakes were never over-exercised. This was good, as they were bad. The rear was actually more powerful than the front and it took me years on other bikes to get out of the habit of relying on the rear and the gearbox to actually slow down. My A65 had the conical (aka comical) hub twin-leading shoe, which on the face of it should have been pretty powerful. But rather than a rod activating the second shoe, a design that had worked perfectly well on a previous generation of BSAs, Nortons and Triumphs, BSA elected to cost-cut by having the brake cable outer activate it by pushing against the cam as the inner pulled the other cam. Cable outers can compress, of course, and when you applied the brake that's exactly what happened. Retardation was minimal, despite putting a fair bit of time and effort into mounting and adjusting both sets of shoes to bite the drum simultaneously

And as if this lack of power wasn't enough, it got very hot as well, despite an air-scoop on the front big enough to swallow sparrows. I remember testing the front brake after meticulously setting it all up: nice straight road somewhere on Anglesey, up to 95mph, apply front brake. Slowly down to 75mph, then they seemed to bite better and speed rapidly came down to about 50mph (though not rapidly enough to provoke any howls from the front tyre). And then they just faded away – lever came back to the handlebars, bike actually felt like she was speeding up and once again I had to resort to the back brake to come to a halt.

Interesting observation, which, bearing in mind others' experiences of the same brake, shows that the only consistent thing about the conical hub front TLS brake is the inconsistent experiences of different riders! More riding (or falling off) impressions:

> Very solidly built though. I'd returned to college minus MOT one September (well, I'd phoned from Hampshire to book the MOT in Wales), and coming into Beaumaris the next day with a Welsh chum on the back, a car turned right as I was overtaking it. I swung right but couldn't avoid it and bounced off the wing, up the pavement, trying to regain control as pedestrians dived for cover and Roland, my pillion, clung on for grim death. But got her back, parked up, inspected the damage (bent left foot peg, scratched clutch lever, sore knee), then limped back to the offending car. Which was a mess. The foot peg had punctured the front offside tyre, my knee had lightly creased the middle of the wing, and the left handlebar and clutch lever had gouged the top of the wing, popping out the headlamp, which lay smashed on the floor. The driver was a tourist, from Liverpool I think, and while none too happy agreed fairly quickly that we'd come out even and to leave it at that; I was lucky that my pillion spoke fluent Welsh (and very volubly now the shock had worn off), so all the witnesses were on my side.

Nick found that the electrics weren't bad either, with none of the usual starting or non-functioning lights that could plague British bikes from that era. He noted that the bike was equipped with:

> . . . a non-standard car type sealed beam front (with no parking light), indicators that worked and Lucas 'butterfly' switchgear, unlabelled, which the press at the time disliked but I had no problems with. Dip and full beam on the left, indicators on the right and two push buttons on either side for the kill switch (this was before the days of positive kill switches), headlamp flash and horn, plus one spare. Funny thing with the headlamp flash was that towards the end the bike definitely went faster with the flash on – I could feel a power increase as I pressed it. Presumably something to do with alternator coils being pulled into service, but I never got to the bottom of the problem.

The bike was stolen shortly after Nick returned home from completing his Welsh studies and was never seen again, which Nick found a real shame. So if anyone out there knows the whereabouts of SWL 877M, engine/frame number A65LG NGOO2255 (he is pretty sure of that number), give him a call. He'd love to see her again and make up for his earlier treatment by

This 1965 Lightning has been given a Spitfire tank and later seat and side panels. This makes for an attractive bike that rides well.

lavishing some proper care and attention on her! Again, these bikes have the 'X factor' that does inspire intense loyalty in their owners.

1965 Lightning – In Spitfire Clothes

Chapter 7 chronicles my restoration of a 1965 A65 Lightning. My experiences of riding the restored bike, however, are detailed here.

First impressions of the machine are that it is compact and that it fits my relatively large frame comfortably. My knees do fit into the recesses in the tank, and the handlebar controls 'fall readily to hand', to quote many of the old road tests. Starting is hampered by the low-geared kick-start, and it takes two or three kicks to get going from cold. The choke mechanism on the

The tickler on the right-hand side Monobloc carburettor is almost impossible to get at with a gloved hand!

The smooth lines of the bike are enhanced by the later tank and side panels. The handling and road holding provided by the all-welded frame and new tyres are impressive.

Monoblocs seems ineffectual at first, but checking and adjusting the cable made sure that the chokes closed completely, and this improved matters considerably. The bike would consistently start on the second kick from cold. Getting at the tickler for the right-hand side is almost impossible as the carburettor is not 'handed', and the two fuel pipes go either side of it, leaving no room for a finger – let alone a gloved finger!

However, once the bike is running, the engine is smooth and responsive, with impressive mid-range torque making gear changing unnecessary except if rapid acceleration is needed. The close-ratio gearbox has its ratios closely stacked together at the top end – this means that bottom gear is quite high and the clutch needs slipping up to 10 to 15mph.

Handling and road holding are both very good. The bike can be laid down in corners easily and it holds its line well. The suspension is pretty good and compliant, and not too hard. The new Japanese Dunlop Gold Seal K70 tyres hold the road very well in wet and dry conditions.

The most interesting thing is the reaction of people to the bike. Many onlookers have said what superb looks the bike has, and many comment on how good BSAs were and how they used to own one. It again goes to show what the public remember about BSAs – the popularity of the marque remains high.

Summary

The one overriding theme that comes out of these interviews with owners is the degree of loyalty that the unit twin engenders in their riders. They have either kept the bikes for a good few years, or would be happy to buy their original one back. All identified a feel-good factor, which resulted from a combination of the looks and power characteristics, and despite some mechanical mayhem, all were satisfied with the reliability and performance – or at least did not blame the bike for the mishaps!

7 Restoration of a 1965 BSA A65 Lightning

Introduction

This chapter is a description of the process of renovation and restoration of a 1965 A65L Lightning. This is not a nuts and bolts description along the lines of 'I next removed the gorbel pin, which was 2 thou undersized and needed to be built up using metal spraying', but rather more of a general narrative of the restoration. It does identify both the generic problems found in restoring a bike several

decades old and the specific issues related to the A50 and A65. Most of all, it is intended to be interesting, enjoyable and informative.

Restoring a bike is a rewarding experience, but needs to be approached with open eyes, and a certain level of resources. In my experience the minimum required is:

● a plan
● a dry and secure working environment

As this book was published, there were still plenty of good bikes around – both in use or for sale. This nice early A65 Star was at the January 2004 Kempton Park Autojumble.

- a selection of good tools
- time.

A restoration doesn't just happen; it needs a certain element of planning. In my experience, the plan does not need to be too detailed – but there are a number of elements that need to be addressed. The plan should include an idea of what work you will do and what work you will farm out to experts. The standard of restoration should be considered – is the result going to be a concours contender, or a good everyday bike? The plan should have a rough order of work, and should identify any critical paths – for example, I like to build up a rolling chassis first and then add bits to it, so rebuilding the wheels are usually the first major job, along with fitting new or 'slave' tyres. This can be done while the frame is away being blasted and powder-coated. Once the frame returns, the wheels and suspension can be quickly fitted, giving a convenient rolling chassis and a major psychological boost, as the collection of scrap metal suddenly starts to look like a bike.

While some restorers will do a 'dry' build of all the components, then dismantle the bike, get all the parts finished (painted, plated and so on) and then do a final reassembly, I have found that I can carry out one 'rolling' rebuild on bikes of the 1960s and 70s. Parts availability for these bikes is pretty good, so there is little need to buy universal fittings and then fettle them to fit, so I tend to do the bike as I go along. I will offer up a part, for example a bracket. If it fits, then I paint if required, and fix it in position. However, major cosmetic items like the petrol tank and side panels are trial fitted before being sent away to be painted! I tend to use stainless steel or chrome mudguards.

The working environment is important, and although many excellent restorations have been carried out in small sheds, a warm, well-lit and well-equipped garage or shed makes the restoration a lot easier. It is important that you have good light, electric power is very useful and the area should be secure.

Information

Information is power – and when restoring a bike, the more information about the target of the restoration you can gather the better. While you could write a book on the subject in its own right, this section provides a brief overview of what can be done and where to get the information.

A good starting point is a workshop manual, but, if possible, this should be complemented by a parts manual or list. While the manual will provide the raw data about the bike, hopefully including dimensions, bearing specifications and so on, the parts manual should provide pictures of sub-assemblies and how they fit together – these are invaluable to identify what is missing and what a missing part should look like. These are available as reprints for the unit twins from the usual retail or mail-order outlets, and original copies can sometimes be found at auto jumbles.

Brochures are always useful to gain an idea of what the manufacturers wanted their bikes to look like, and indeed what your restoration may be aiming for. Original brochures are available on the auto-jumble circuit and some specialist booksellers stock them.

Original magazines from the period, such as the *Motor Cycle*, can provide road tests and articles on specific models. Many of these have been reprinted by the Brooklands range of publications. The 'modern' classic magazines, in the UK *Classic Bike*, *The Classic Motorcycle* and *Classic Bike Guide* (which are available in the US), have many articles on all aspects of classic bikes and again provide archive and back issue services. Books on your chosen marque may be available new or second-hand.

Owners' clubs often have library services that can provide access to hard to find archive documents, model specialists for specific advice and other services such as dating information to confirm the age and specification of the machine. In the UK, dating information can assist in recovering a registration number or getting an age-related registration from the national licensing authority, the DVLA.

Sources of information are many and varied. Pictured is an assortment of documents and books of relevance to the BSA Unit Twins.

So research is important and time spent initially researching what is needed will pay dividends. Gathering the information needed to research a project can be almost as much fun as carrying out the project itself – and it is certainly nicer in some ways to be curled up in front of the fire on a cold winter's evening researching a colour scheme or mechanical specification than to be down the garden in an unheated workshop!

Tools and Equipment

Tools are important. A set of relevant spanners (Whitworth and AF), a decent socket set and quality screwdrivers are the basics. Good quality is the key here. There is no point in buying poor quality tools, especially screwdrivers, as they will not last or take any sort of abuse. I can guarantee that you will have to resort to the hammer and chisel at some time in any restoration! Heat is useful in helping to minimize this type of abuse – a good blowtorch can help with shifting the most stubborn of fasteners, as will an impact driver.

A set of taps and dies and some bar stock can save time if a specific fastener is needed – you can make one rather then having to go out and buy it. On the BSA A65 the early machines were made with a variety of thread forms, including BSF (British Standard Fine), BSC (British Standard Coarse) and Cycle (CEI), and then during the late 1960s the factory moved towards standardizing on the US UNF (Unified Fine) and UNC (Unified Coarse). However, the changeover was never completed, resulting in an interesting assortment of fastening on the later machines!

Most bikes will also have a number of special tools available for them – some will be necessary, some can be improvised. The A65 workshop manual identifies that the following tools are required:

- valve seat cutter (61-3293, 61-3299, 61-3290)
- valve grinding tool (61-5035)
- gudgeon bush extractor/fitting tool (61-3652)★

- piston ring slippers (61-3682, 61-3707)
- contact breaker cam extractor (61-5005)★
- valve guide fitting and extracting punch (61-3382)
- valve spring compressor (61-3341)
- tappet circlip fitting tool (61-3702)★
- crankshaft balance weights (61-3710, 61-3711)★
- universal pinion extractor (61-3676)
- clutch sleeve extractor (61-3766)★
- camshaft bush extractor (61-3159)★
- clutch nut screwdriver (61-3767)★
- clutch locking tool (61-3768)★
- steering head adjusting tool (61-3008)★
- damper dismantling and assembly tool (61-3503)★
- fork leg fitting and removal tool (61-3350)★
- oil seal holder fitting and removal tool (61-3005)★
- oil seal extractor punch (61-3006)★
- oil seal assembly tool (61-3007)★
- fork damper rod recovery tool (61-3765)★.

Those with an asterisk are BSA specific tools; the rest are standard automotive tools. It should be noted that none of these specific tools is vital, as it is often possible to improvise an alternative, or make a replacement. However, use of the specific tool does make the job easier and quicker – and saves the time needed to make up an alternative.

Sourcing of Spares

There are several ways of sourcing spares. Firstly, there is your local bike shop – and if you don't use it, then don't moan if it goes out of business. Secondly, there is mail order – this can be excellent or dire depending on the shop and you can only find out the hard way! Thirdly, there are auto jumbles, where new and second-hand spares are about but may take some time to find.

The local bike shop, if you are lucky, will have enthusiastic and knowledgeable staff, who can be invaluable in assisting you in a rebuild, as well as giving advice. Sometimes it is worth taking your problems to them rather than a list of parts, to see what they recommend – for example, a solid-state regulator/rectifier may be cheaper than a new zener diode, heat sink and rectifier, and will be more reliable. You can see the goods before you buy, and can come in with a grime-encrusted part and mutter 'Got one of these?' or 'What's this then?' with some possibility of a sensible answer. Spend enough time and money there and you may qualify for a free cup of tea!

Mail order may be the only alternative for those hard to find spares, or for those people without a local classic bike shop. Some traders are good, and will send off your order on the day it was received, but that may not always be the case. The disadvantage of mail order is that you can't see the goods, it can be inconvenient to return them if they are not satisfactory, and postage charges can be steep. Also make sure that prices quoted include the sales tax (VAT in the UK) and the postage charge. A good strategy is to use only a couple of mail-order outlets. Try those advertised in the classic bike press, and if using them for the first time, I suggest you try a small order to 'test the waters'. If the order is processed promptly and the spares are of the requisite quality then continue to use them – you will build up a good relationship with them as they recognize you as a valued customer. If the initial order is slow in delivery or of unsatisfactory quality, then don't use them again. One thing that I find annoying is when you order a part, then it doesn't arrive, and you ring back to find that such and such is out of stock and they are waiting for it to be ordered – always check if possible that the parts ordered are available, and, if not, agree a policy with the vendor for sending part of the overall order. There is nothing more annoying than having a rebuild held up because of the lack of a critical part in an order that has not been sent because some other part, not on your critical path, was not in stock at the time!

Auto jumbles should be treated as a good day out, with the benefit of possibly getting some spares thrown in! If you have an obscure part you want to match, then take it along – it's better to compare than rely on memory. Cables are a case in point, as you can compare the lengths of the inner and outer with the new item. Be careful

with second-hand spares – they may be good only for scrap. Beware of loosely assembled components like forks that look complete – chances are they have been slung together out of a random selection of semi-matching parts. But, conversely, if the price is right and you only need some bits, then buy the whole assembly. The other bits may come in useful one day, or may form the basis for your own debut as an auto-jumble trader when you need to clear some room in the workshop. Quite a few reputable dealers attend auto jumbles and this can be a good way of saving postage – put in an order and pick it up at your local jumble. Another plus of auto jumbles is the number of bikes that there are in the car park – not only does this provide a free bike show in its own right, but if you have a problem in working out how a component is supposed to fit, then inspection of the relevant bike may provide the answer.

There is one more source of spares; that is, the friends, acquaintances and owners' club, described by Royce Creasley in the 1970s *Bike* magazine as the Cosmic Spares Supplier. It can be quite amazing how the spare part (or even the bike) you've been scouring the country for can be unearthed by a chance remark at a local run or owners' club night.

The Plan

A restoration starts with a visual inspection and assessment, to identify what is missing and what is worn out or broken and needs replacing. The engine, gearbox and primary drive are inspected, including checking oil filters and drain plugs for evidence of any actual or impending mechanical mayhem. At this stage, a decision can be taken as to whether the engine should be started.

After the initial inspection, the restoration proper can begin. The overall restoration plan on the Lightning A65 below was to break up the bike into its major components and tackle them one at a time. I don't do paint (apart from small black brackets!) and always farm out the preparation and painting of the frame, tank, side panels

As bought, this Lightning A65 was largely complete, but had a number of non-standard parts. The chrome on the wheels, headlamp and mudguards was all poor, and the front mudguard was definitely not right.

and mudguards. Any major engineering work such as crank grinding and reboring is also farmed out at this stage.

The first job is to get the frame stripped down, shot blasted and powder coated, and while that is being done the wheels can be rebuilt, and the brakes and suspension serviced. Once the frame is back, a rolling chassis can be built. Then the engine and gearbox can be rebuilt, and installed in the rolling chassis. Ancillary components, such as mudguards, can be sourced in the meantime, and installed as and when they arrive. Rewiring can also take place. The petrol tank will be sent out for re-chroming

or a better second-hand one will be located. The petrol tank and side panels will also need to be sent out for final painting. Obviously, they will be the last things to be replaced on the machine!

The Bike as Found

The subject of this restoration is a 1965 BSA A65 Lightning. It was bought as a non-runner, restoration project, which at first glance looked to be almost complete. Most of the main components were fitted and the bike could be wheeled about. The brakes worked, the exhaust system was complete and looked reusable. The

The whole bike was loosely assembled, with some evidence of work done on it. All of the basics were present, which is important in a restoration.

tank was in primer and the side panels were very tatty. The bike generally looked well used, but near complete and standard.

The initial inspection of the machine resulted in the following observations:

- *Engine* While the engine did turn over, there was evidence of some loosely assembled parts, such as the rocker cover. At least one head bolt was missing. The carburettors were loosely fitted, and the clutch cable was in poor condition. The rear engine plates were loose. There was no oil in the oil tank, and the oil feed pipes were disconnected. On the basis of this, it appeared that the engine had been hurriedly refitted to the frame, and its condition was poor. I did not attempt to start it.
- *Frame* While the paint on the frame was not too bad, there were enough odd rust spots and bare patches to justify blasting and refinishing. The centre stand was fitted and appeared to have new fixings. There was no side stand

fitted, but there was a B40 type with flat 'foot' present in a box of spares.
- *Suspension (front forks)* There were no headlamp 'ears' to support the headlight, only a pair of period John Tickle after-market brackets. All three of the fork yoke top nuts had damaged chrome and were rusty and rounded. The steering damper was fitted and working, but the steering head bearings seemed a bit notchy, so would need to be replaced. The fork stanchions ('shaft' in the BSA parts manual) were rusty and needed replacing. The fork springs appeared to be too short, as they were loose and could be moved up and down when the bike was on its centre stand.
- *Suspension (rear swinging arm)* While the swinging arm bearings were good, because they were metalastic they would need to come out and be replaced when the frame was blasted and powder-coated, as the heat from the powder coating process could affect them. The rear shock absorbers were standard

Closer examination exposed the correct (for a 1965 Lightning) open-ended frame. The oil tank was the only thing under the seat, and the electrics were non-existent.

Girling fully shrouded types and looked reasonable; they appeared to have satisfactory springing and damping when tested statically. The chain guard was loose and looked to have been modified in the past, and its fixings needed looking at.

- *Wheels and brakes* The front wheel rim needed replacing due to lifting chrome, and the rear rim, while not as bad as the front, was also on the way out. All the spokes were rusty and many were loose. Both brakes appeared to be in good working order, as were the hubs and wheel bearings. The rear sprocket and chain also seemed to be in good condition.

- *Mudguards* The front mudguard was in good condition but was incorrect and did not fit properly. Conversely, the rear mudguard was original but very rusty and probably needed replacing.

- *Tinware* The toolbox/battery carrier/oil tank were all there, including the toolkit zip-up case. Surprisingly, there was no corrosion evident on the battery carrier, which was unpainted and looked like a new pattern part. There were no fixings either with the carrier – it was loose in the box of bits.

- *Petrol tank/side panels* Both needed refinishing. The tank was in primer, with the correct quick release 'winged' filler cap, but the chrome under the primer was poor, and several of the badge and knee grip screw holes had rusted-in screws. The side panels themselves were the correct glass-fibre. They had been painted at least twice, if not three times. Currently they were a bilious yellow, which I imagine was the Dulux match for the BSA Gold paint that would have been the original colour of a 1965 Lightning. The front fitting bar for the side panels that bolts on to the frame ahead of the oil tank was missing.

- *Seat* This was in good condition, albeit a later (1966 on) hump-back affair. While it was not new, the cover had no tears, the base was rust-free, the plastic chrome strip around the bottom edge was good and the fixing bolt holes still had their threads intact. All it needed was a clean.

- *Electrics (including lights)* The wiring loom was useless, with numerous bodges, missing connectors and damaged insulation. There was no rectifier or battery. The headlamp shell had poor chrome and would need replacing, but the rim should clean up. The headlight glass was good, but the reflector was very dull. The rear light assembly and number plate mount were original but needed a clean-up and paint, and a new lens. There was no dip/horn switch, but the original ignition and light switches in the headlamp appeared good, and were complete with their associated sockets. The ammeter in the headlamp needed testing, but did not look too bad.

- *Instruments* The speedometer and tachometer both appeared to work, and were tested by inserting a short piece of broken speedometer cable in them and rotating. Both their chrome bezels needed cleaning. The instrument carrier pods both needed repainting. New rubbers were needed to mount the instruments in the pods as the originals were badly perished.

- *Handlebars and controls* The handlebars were very rusty and needed replacement. The brake and clutch levers appeared to be the alloy Gold Star type with 'star' cable adjusters and just needed a good polish. All cables were worn, with damage to the outers – most would need replacement.

In addition, the bike came with a box of assorted parts, brackets, electrical components and assorted odds and ends.

The main obvious missing parts were therefore the headlight supports (or fork sleeves as BSA called them), although as the rebuild progressed more missing parts would be discovered. Parts eventually found to be needing replacement included the front and rear mudguards, headlamp shell and rim, the majority of the electrical system (including a new wiring loom) and the front and rear wheel rims and all the spokes. The front forks needed some investigation, and the engine, while appearing complete, turned out to be suspect.

It was not the intention to restore the bike to concours condition, or to be totally original. Rather I aimed to create a usable classic, incorporating at least a later 12V electrical system and electronic ignition. The finish would include powder coating of the frame, galvanized wheel spokes and chrome rims.

The list above was an initial assessment. As I detail each of the following sections, more items will be found wanting and will be addressed. The initial assessment gave me a starting point, from which I deduced that the bike was worth restoring.

Preparing the Rolling Chassis

Frame and Swinging Arm

Before stripping down, the frame was checked for alignment and it appeared to be straight. Stripping down of the various components was straightforward, with the exception of the removal of the swinging arm. The swinging arm pivots around two silentbloc rubber bushes (made up of a steel outer bush, a rubber insert and steel inner bush), and if the frame and swinging arm are to be stove-enamelled or powder-coated, then they would need to be separated. There are two reasons for this – firstly, I did not know if the baking process used would ruin the rubbers in the bushes, and was not prepared to find out, and secondly it is the only way to get a proper job done.

In the case of this bike, the bushes were seized on to the swinging arm spindle through corrosion, and the only way to remove the swinging arm from the frame was to drive out the spindle. Penetrating oil was the first line of attack. Heat may work, but will melt the rubber bushes, and may not free the bush inner steel races from the spindle. The swinging arm bush inners are too big to pass through the holes in the frame. Therefore it is necessary to cut off the ends of the spindle between the frame plates if possible – if there is not enough room then the ends outside of the frame are cut off and the ends of the spindle cut or ground down enough to allow the swinging arm to be removed from the frame. The silentbloc inners and the spindle are easily removed by heating until the rubbers let go, leaving the inners still attached to the butchered spindle, and all only fit for the scrap bin. This leaves the outer bearing in the swinging arm. If the bike is original there will also be a spacer tube between the two bushes. To remove the outer bushes, use a punch or chisel to force the bush away from the swinging arm by collapsing the bush in on itself. This will both distort the bush and help to break the corrosion that has glued it to the swinging arm. Once the bush has collapsed all the way round, use a drift to punch it out from the other end. This worked for me – trying to cut the bushes out with a cold chisel and hacksaw took a very long time compared to the first method!

New bushes are inserted by pressing them into the swinging arm. I used a length of threaded rod with a nut, a suitable sized socket

which bears on the bush on one end and a big flat washer on the other end to bear against the swinging arm. Winding in the nut pushes the bearing into the swinging arm. When inserting the new bushes, be careful to use a circular drift (a socket is ideal) that is large enough to bear on the outer 'race' of the bush. If your drift or socket is smaller than the outer bush the apparatus will simply push the inner bush out of the outer bush, thereby wrecking it. These bushes can be very tight, so it helps to shrink the bush by putting it in the freezer for a while – heating the swinging arm would also help, but would not do the shiny new paint much good.

Footrest attachments are handed – the left-hand footrest stud has a left-hand thread, the right-hand footrest has a right-hand thread. Presumably this was to prevent the footrest nuts undoing themselves due to vibration, as the footrests themselves fit on to a taper to allow them to be adjusted. The footrests on the project as found were fastened on with bolts – and the left-hand one had a right-handed thread. Luckily this bolt had only been forced in by a couple of threads and was smaller than standard, so the

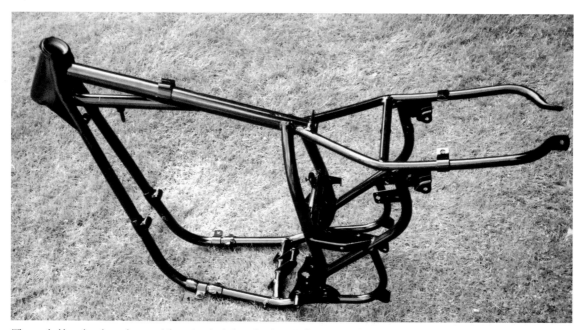

The newly blasted and powder-coated frame just back from the shop. Make sure you do any frame repairs needed before this stage!

thread was easily recovered with the correct stud. The right-hand footrest only needed a new stud and washer to be fitted. Note that with a powder-coated or newly painted frame you will need to clean the paint off of the taper, otherwise your footrests will droop as soon as any weight is placed on them.

Forks

The top nuts and centre yoke nut were all heavily corroded and beyond saving, so new ones were bought. The first problem on the forks was obtaining the correct headlamp brackets. Initially I bought a pair that was in fact too long to fit. On further investigation it appeared that the 1965 Lightning had different top yokes to the following year's models, in that the 1965 top yokes' outer edges drop down below the level of the centre by about 2cm – distinguishable from the later yokes as the handlebar mounting are in front of the steering damper. Buying the correct brackets (part numbers 68-5059 and 68-5060) solved this problem, as they are shorter than the later items (part numbers 68-5176 and 68-5177).

Then another problem emerged when I assembled the forks as a dry run. I found the stanchions that were fitted to the bike as bought were later types, which were slightly longer than the originals to take into account the flat yokes. The early stanchions are 21.2in long (Part number 68-5030), while the later stanchions are 2.5in longer at 23.7in (Part Number 68-5144) – this was the reason for the springs appearing to be too short in the initial assessment. So a pair of new early stanchions was added to the shopping list, to go with the new headlamp brackets, chromed spring holders, new chrome top nuts, chrome yoke nut, new bushes and seals already bought. One of the old fork top nuts was used to form the basis of a fork leg fitting and removal tool. This comprised a length of steel rod, approximately 12in, threaded at both ends. The fork top nut had the hexagon ground or filed off, and a hole drilled in the middle. The steel rod was bolted into this hole, and locked in position using two nuts, and a handle was made

up to fit on the other end from a length of alloy rod, about 1in in diameter. When refitting the stanchions, the tool is threaded into the stanchion top, and then the stanchion can be pulled up into the top yoke. It can then be held by doing up the bottom yoke pinch bolts. You can then remove the tools and screw in the top nut. Finally, once the front wheel has been fitted, release the pinch bolts and bounce the bike on the suspension before finally retightening the pinch bolts and then the top nuts. The original way of doing this without the factory tool was to use a household broom handle – many mothers must have been puzzled by the appearance of threads on the broom handle!

Wheels, Brakes and Tyres

The front wheel rim chrome was rusty and lifting, and was beyond recovery so needed to be replaced. The rear rim, while looking super-ficially reasonable, was also too far gone to respond to chrome polish, so also needed replacing. All the spokes were rusty, so again had to be replaced. Rechroming of rims seems to be a contentious issue – some chromers will rechrome, some will not. There are two issues here. Firstly, the spoke holes in the rim can tear the chromer's polishing mops, and secondly the area under the turned-over edge of the rim cannot be cleaned, so if corrosion is present, then it cannot be removed. I decided not to get the originals rechromed for these reasons and two more – cost and availability. New rims were available and were cheaper than restoring the originals. So new Italian chrome rims and galvanized spokes were bought and the wheels built up using a homemade jig and a Black & Decker workmate.

There were no problems found with either the front or rear hubs. The BSA 'crinkle' rear hub was riveted together by the factory, and these rivets can loosen off, leading to the two outer sections becoming loose on the inner sleeve, but they were fine on this example. There seem to be no known faults on the front hub, which I inspected for flaws and found to be satisfactory. The wheel bearings front and rear were inspected and found to be serviceable, so were cleaned and repacked with grease.

The tyres were replaced as a matter of course with a set of Dunlop K70s. Dunlop is still producing these classic tyres, although they are actually made in Japan – somewhat ironic considering the poor performance of the Japanese tyres produced in the 1960s. They are identical to the original equipment K70s in appearance, but benefit from current tyre compound technology. In my experience, these Japanese Dunlop tyres perform much better than the British originals in terms of grip, wet weather performance and wear. New inner tubes and rim tapes were used – again, it is a false economy and potentially dangerous to reuse these components if you do not know their history.

Handlebar Controls and Control Cables

The brake lever and clutch levers were of the alloy Gold Star type, with the brass four-pointed 'star' type of adjuster. When cleaned up, it became apparent that the levers were not a perfect match to the handlebar clamps, and with a cable installed it was clear that the marriage was not one made in heaven. Cleaning out the

cable nipple hole in the lever and lubricating the cable nipple helped to solve the apparent mismatch, and comparison with a second-hand lever assembly revealed that they were not too different. The final result was not perfect, and I suspect that the original levers have been replaced at some stage, but since being cleaned up and lubricated they do work nicely and are acceptable.

Surprisingly, the control cables were probably the hardest parts to find. This was caused by a combination of the myriad types of BSA cable made at the time, and the fact that the alloy levers on the Lightning did not have the adjusters built into the cables – unlike the standard steel BSA levers of the time. One set of brake and clutch cables bought from a cable specialist at an auto jumble proved to be completely wrong in both end fittings and the difference in length between the inner/outer, and this was despite the dealer being given the exact model details. While I should have recognized that the end fitting was not right, the cable lengths are difficult to assess or measure unless the cable specification is available to you. In this case, it's usually best to get your money back and go to a different source for the cable.

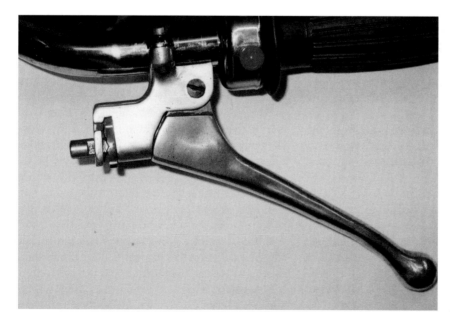

The Gold Star type alloy levers do not match perfectly with their handlebar mounts. However, they do work well in practice.

Throttle cables were non-standard, as I was using a twin cable twist grip. I made these up to length from new, soldering the nipples on using silver solder, not commercial electrical solder. The choke cables were the only reusable cables that came with the bike.

Mudguards

The chrome on the rear mudguard was shot. A replacement was sourced from Burton Bike Bits, who are remanufacturing these parts. It was pre-drilled and fitted without any need for modifications. It should be remembered that there was a large number of variants of rear mudguards, due to the different positionings of the fixing holes used for the various variants of the range. It is best to buy from a knowledgeable supplier to ensure that you get the correct one for your particular model and year. If possible, take along the original to compare.

On fitting the replacement reproduction chromed rear mudguard, an assembly quirk of the A50/A65 range reared its head – you cannot fit the oil tank or the toolbox pressing with the mudguard in place. I became quite adept at removing the mudguard as I discovered the correct assembly sequence for these components – it is oil tank, toolbox, then mudguard!

The original rear light and number plate fitting was cleaned up, repainted using Finnegan's Smoothite black paint, and fitted to the new mudguard. The unit fitted perfectly to the pre-drilled holes in the mudguard. The rear mudguard support loop was also repainted and refitted.

The chrome front mudguard that came with the bike appeared to be an after-market pattern part or possibly a late 1960s Triumph/BSA type. Its fixings were wrong, although with some invention the various stays that came with the bike could be and were pressed into service. However, the finished result did not look original and was not really an improvement, so it was replaced with a new pattern item, again from Burton Bike Bits. New, correct pattern front and rear stays and the centre flat fixings were also bought from Burton, and the complete assembly bolted on, to provide an original and attractive front end.

Engine and Gearbox

The first stage in the engine rebuild was to assess its condition by stripping it down and inspecting it. To do this, it is necessary to be both methodical and careful. The engine can be broken into four units, each of which can be addressed separately. These are the top end (cylinder head and barrels and pistons), the primary drive, the engine bottom end (crank, connecting rods, oil pump and camshaft) and the gearbox. Unfortunately, on the unit twins, any bottom end work on the engine's crankshaft involves splitting the crankcases, and this requires the top end and primary drive to be dismantled and the engine removed from the frame.

Engine – Top End

Once the engine was out of the frame, removal of the rocker cover (which was helped by the fact that it only had half its nuts present) revealed one cylinder head bolt missing. This was not a good sign as to the overall state of the engine! Once the rocker box was off, the rocker shafts were removed by loosening the nuts of the timing side and drifting them out. There are two things to watch – the spacers and spring washers present on the shaft position the rockers, so make a note of which were where, then check in the manual to see if the previous owner had put them back correctly the last time the head was off. Secondly, only drift out the rocker shaft while there is no pressure being exerted on the shaft by the pushrods – rotate the engine to get clearance on both of the valves serviced by the shaft! There should be a split pin in the end of the rocker oil feed between the two inlet valves. This pin is there to ensure that the feed remains clear, and acts as a regulator for the flow of oil.

Once the rocker shafts and associated rockers have been removed, the centre five cylinder head bolts become accessible. Do not miss the single bolt recessed in the pushrod tunnel between the two cylinders. The bolts and the four outer nuts should be eased off in the sequence described in the manual to avoid distorting the head. Once all nine fasteners have been removed the head can be taken off, probably with the assistance of a block of wood and a hammer. Careful use of this equipment will be fine – careless use will result in damage, probably broken fins. Never lever between the head and barrels, as you will break a fin or wreck the mating surface. If the head will not move, then check all nine fixings have been removed, then try again. A sharp tap with the hammer and block of wood on the bottom of the exhaust port sometimes helps. If the previous owner has used some particularly evil jointing compound or corrosion has firmly fixed the head and barrels together, then try turning the engine over. The compression may blow the join; some oil down the plughole will also assist. Heating the cylinder head/barrel join with a blowtorch may also help. Finally, if all else fails remove the four outer studs from the barrel and try the block of wood and hammer routine horizontally – the join may break in shear easier than in tension. If there is still no joy, remove the complete top end by taking the barrel off and take it to your local engineering company! In this particular case, as in most cases, the head came off with gentle use of the block of wood and some wriggling.

Once the joint has been broken, the head may be stiff to remove as it has to clear the four outer studs and these may not be completely true, but gentle persuasion applied evenly all the way round the head will work. Hitting the head with a hammer or levering between the head and barrel will result in broken fins, so care is needed!

Upon removal, the head in this case was found to contain two very new looking exhaust valves and was very clean, with little carbon build-up.

Removal of the barrels is simply a matter of undoing the eight nuts around the periphery, and gently tapping with a block of wood to break the join. Again, be careful where you tap – although the barrel is made of cast iron and the fins are more robust than those on the head, they are brittle and will break if hit too hard. The nuts may not have enough clearance to come off completely, but once the barrel has been moved up a bit they can be removed completely. Again, never lever between the barrel and crankcase – if the barrels are not moving there is something wrong, most likely a missed fastener.

The pistons were also clean, and had some minor witness marks where the exhaust valves had hit them, which probably explained the new valves. The marks were not bad enough to scrap the pistons. There did not appear to be any size

The barrels were already bored out to +040 thou, but were in good shape. Note the row of four tappets at the rear, the four outer studs and five bolt holds for the head.

markings stamped on the pistons; however, close inspection revealed +040, indicating that the pistons were on the second oversize. Measuring of the barrels indicated that they were also +040 oversize, and within tolerances for the size. The bores were in good condition, with no scores or scrapes, and no ridge at the top of the bore to indicate excessive wear, so the way ahead was to replace the piston rings only and a new set of rings were duly purchased.

The valves were removed and, bearing in mind the witness marks on the pistons, were checked to see if they were straight. Valve springs were measured to ensure that they were in tolerance. There are two springs per valve, an inner and outer. Their correct lengths are given in the workshop manual. Valves and springs were found to be in good condition, as were the valve guides. The valves were ground in using fine grinding paste, and then reassembled in the head. The small ends were checked and there was no play.

Primary Drive

In order to dismantle the primary drive, the first thing to do is to remove the alternator stator, held on with three nuts. The rotor nut is removed after locking up the primary drive – I use a chunk of wood in the primary chain and clutch. Then, using a universal puller, pull the rotor off of the crankshaft. Lifting the rotor with a spanner will test the state of the magnets in the stator – if each of the magnets bonded into the edge of the stator can support its weight then the alternator should work. The other point to inspect is to ensure that the centre of the rotor is still bonded to the outer – strange rumblings that sound like main bearings going can occur if the outer is loose on the inner.

Removing the clutch, drive chain and engine sprocket should be done in one go. Remove the clutch springs and pressure plate, and then take out the clutch plates. A magnetic pick-up tool (available from all good auto jumbles!) can help in removing the plates. Then undo the clutch centre nut – to do this you need to lock the clutch inner to the outer, and you can use either

the correct tool, make your own tool using two clutch plates (one friction, one drive) bolted together with a handle fixed on, or use a suitable large washer between the slots on the clutch centre and the basket and lock the primary chain to the clutch basket using a block of wood. Once the centre nut is off, then it is best to use the correct tool to pull the clutch hub off of its tapered shaft. The clutch and primary drive sprocket should then be taken off as one – the chain does not (or should not!) bend enough to allow removal of one or the other. A puller may be needed to take the engine sprocket off of the crank. As the engine sprocket has holes drilled and tapped, a puller can be improvised using a steel bar and two long bolts; otherwise a universal puller can be used.

Gearbox

Initial pushing backwards and forwards of the Lightning A65 when collected showed that all the gears were present, although the gear lever return spring was obviously not working. This was confirmed when the outer timing cover was removed and one half of the spring fell out. Once the clutch has been loosened from the mainshaft, the gearbox can be extracted from its case in the timing side still attached to its circular plate. The gearbox and change mechanism is self-contained on this plate, making it very easy to dismantle and reassemble, especially when compared to the equivalent Triumph.

The outer casing appeared untouched, and the gears inside showed little, if any, wear. All teeth were present on all the gears, the dogs that engage the gears were unworn – if the edges of the dogs, or the holes into which the dogs engage, are radiused or worn, then the gear will likely jump out of engagement under load. Gearbox bearings and bushes were similarly unworn, so the whole lot was put back into its casing in the timing-side crankcase.

Engine – Bottom End

Taking off the sump filter will usually expose any major engine problems – this is where the swarf and alloy particles of a soon-to-explode engine will be gathered. It has to come off if you are splitting the cases, but it is worth putting it back on to the timing-side case to protect the scavenge pipe. While looking, it is well worth checking that the ball bearing that sits in the scavenge pipe is still there and loose – this helps to prevent wet sumping.

Note the camshaft and engine pinion nut on the timing side have left hand threads. The crankshaft pinion can be carefully levered off the crankshaft with two large screwdrivers if the BSA tool is not available.

If the oil pump is a dull grey it has been cast from alloy and probably distorted – see how easy it is to turn by hand. In this case, there was a definite tight spot, so the intention was to replace it with a cast iron bodied version. However, at the time of writing, new pumps were found to be unobtainable. The existing pump was therefore stripped down and inspected. Very little wear was found, with slight scoring on the end plate being the only visible sign. This was lapped back, and the pump reassembled. The pump body was checked for distortion across the face that fits to the crankcases, and none was discernible. So the pump was reused, although a lookout for a new component will be maintained.

Before splitting the crankcases, it is worth checking the crankshaft end float. This is the amount of sideways movement that the crank has when in the cases. The engine is particularly sensitive to end float, which should be around 2–3 thou only – any more than this and the drive-side main bearing will suffer. End float on the engine was in the region of 15–20 thou on this engine, which was a case for concern. Once the cases had been split there was no apparent reason for the excessive end float – both main bearings were not badly worn, although the shims between the crankshaft and the drive-side main bearing were badly battered and beginning to break up. Note that on the A50/A65 it is possible to split the crankcases without disturbing the gearbox.

Once the crankcases had been split, the crank was removed for inspection, and this also exposed the main bearings for scrutiny. Replacement of the mains required heating the cases to about 200°C – this enabled both the timing-side bush and the outer race of the two-part drive-side roller to be easily removed, and new ones inserted. If the timing-side bush has to be replaced it will need to be line-reamed to fit the crank – check with your local bike shop for a

The timing-side crankcase with the new main bearing installed. The bush has been line-reamed to size.

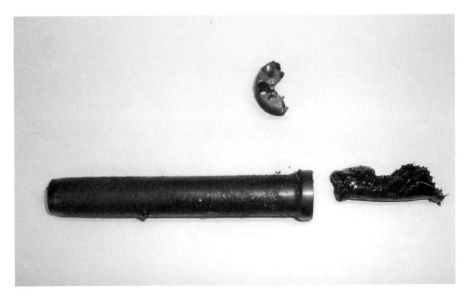

suitable engineering shop to do this, as it is a precision operation.

While that is being done, the big-end journals and timing-side journal should be reground if they need it – obviously this will dictate what undersize of timing-side bush is required. While the crank is out, even if the journals do not need grinding the sludge trap should be cleaned out. This is a hollow tube in the crank that runs through both big-end journals. It is an essential part of the oiling system, and its function is to trap sludge and debris before they get to the big ends. Eventually, the tube will fill up with sludge, which cuts off the oil supply to the big ends. This was the first unfortunate aspect of the design; the second was the use of a slotted plug to seal the tube off – this is usually impossible to remove without resorting to brute force, impact drivers, drills and other types of mechanical butchery. Luckily, the plug can be replaced (and will probably need to be anyway) with one with a hexagonal hole which can be removed next time cleanly with a large Allen key.

The camshaft can also be left in the timing-side case. In the end of the camshaft bearing in the drive-side case there should be a spring and a timed rotary breather that is driven by a slot on the end of the camshaft. These will invariably fall out when the crankcases are split, and then roll off the bench on to the floor – in different directions. Care must be taken when reassembling the crankcases that the rotary valve is properly engaged in the camshaft. This can be achieved by sticking the breather disc and spring to the end of the camshaft with grease before finally putting the crankcases back together.

Reassembly of the crank in the crankcases is a fiddly job, as the correct amount of end float must be achieved by shimming the drive-side main bearing inner race on the crank. This means that once the new mains are installed in the cases one or more trial assemblies need to be carried out – with a supply of shims (Triumph T140 shims can be used). The drive-side main inner race should be carefully pressed into position on the crank, and the crank and cases then assembled. It is worth placing a shim of known size behind the bearing, as it will make it easier to pull the bearing off the crank once the correct shim size has been determined. The cases are then bolted together tightly. Then the end float of the crank can be checked. A dial gauge is the best method to use, but with care a pointer can be rigged up on one of the alternator studs and the end float measured with feeler gauges. Once the end float is determined, the appropriate thickness of shims required can be calculated to allow the required amount: .0015

The crank with its flywheel as returned from the shop. The two big-end journals and the timing-side main journal have all been reground.

to .003in (1.5 to 3 thousandths of an inch) for a 1965 engine (but check this value for specific motors, as the tolerance does depend on the year of the motor) and the crankcases are then split. The drive-side main needs to be carefully removed from the crank and the appropriate size of shim inserted. Then put the bearing back, and carry out the process again – if you are skilful (or lucky) the end float will be correct; if not, repeat the process until it is right.

The crankshaft was measured up and found to need both big ends and the timing-side journal regrinding. This meant fitting a new undersize timing-side bush (+020 thou) and big-end shells (+030 thou). While the drive-side main bearing appeared to be in good condition, it was decided to replace it as well while the cases were split. The new timing-side bush needed to be reamed to fit the newly ground journal once it was fitted in the crankcase half. This operation and the regrinding of the crank were entrusted to a local engineering company.

The bore in the barrels showed no signs of scoring or obvious wear, and this was confirmed by measurement. The barrels were, however, +040 thou oversized. New rings were procured.

Rebuilding the engine was straightforward, once the above process to ensure correct crankshaft end float had been completed. The bottom half of the engine, including the gearbox, oil pump and cam drive and the primary drive, was built up on the bench. The pistons and barrels were fitted, and the outer cases were fitted. The engine was then lifted into the frame and all of the engine bolts and the rear engine plates were loosely bolted in place. Once all of the engine mounting bolts were in place they could be bolted in and tightened down. If this process is not followed, and engine bolts are put in and tightened one by one, then it is almost guaranteed that the final couple of bolts will not line up with the frame and engine holes.

Once the engine was in the frame the head was replaced. The new solid copper head gasket was annealed by heating it up to red hot and allowing it to cool. This process softens the copper, allowing it to seal the join better. When annealing, the copper article can also be quenched, by dipping it while hot into cold water. Heating then quenching will also get rid of any impurities that are present on the surface of the copper. Head bolts and nuts were tightened to the correct torque settings (see the workshop manual) and the rocker shafts and pushrods could then be replaced, and the tappets set. The rocker box had its studs replaced with new as the threads on some were worn, and was put back in. This completed the rebuilding of the engine.

As the engine goes back together, this is a shot of the newly assembled cases from the timing side. Note the crank and main bush at the front, and the circular gearbox plate to the rear.

One problem did arise after the engine had been put back into the frame. The speedometer drive in the timing-side inner cover was not disturbed during the engine rebuild, and only given a cursory inspection – it turned and had a hole in the end for the speedometer cable. This proved to be a mistake. As the ancillaries were being connected, the new speedometer cable would not fit very far into the drive, and on close inspection the drive was found to have the remains of a cable embedded in it – just far enough down the hole not to be obvious. Luckily, the drive can be extracted from the timing cover while the engine is still in the frame, but getting the broken cable end out proved to be rather awkward. After poking around with fine picks, I had to drill out the cable using a pillar drill, making sure that the

square section of the hole was not compromised by too big a drill.

Oil Filtration

Once the engine was in place, it was possible to determine where and how the non-standard full-flow cartridge oil filter could be fitted. The oil filter unit chosen was the one fitted as standard to the Norton Commando, which is reasonably priced and easy to fit. This comprised an alloy fitting which has pipes for the oil feed in and out, and which the filter is screwed on to. The filter itself was a standard car type spin-on filter (for a Citroën 2CV), so replacements should be readily available and cheap for the foreseeable future.

There is a good-sized gap to the rear of the engine below the swinging arm pivot, and the rear of the engine is where the oil feed pipes are positioned, so this is an ideal location for the filter. The filter fitting had two tapped holes in it at right angles to the oil pipe connections, which were used to fix it to the bottom flat of a U-shaped bracket, made up of 3mm aluminium sheet. This bracket had two holes drilled in the 'legs' of the U, which were bolted to each side of the rear engine mounting bolt. This allowed the filter fitting to mount horizontally with the filter itself sitting below the fitting, where it is easy to access for changes.

The oil return feed was then routed from the engine into the filter, then out to the oil tank. The filter adds about 250cc to the oil capacity, and should help to protect the vulnerable timing-side bearing from any abrasive particles. On fitting a new filter, it is useful to prime the filter by filling it with oil before fitting.

Carburettors

Both carburettors were stripped down and cleaned. The Amal Monobloc was a lot more substantial than the later Amal Concentric and seems to wear a lot less. Older Concentrics invariably have worn and distorted bodies, necessitating replacement if they are to work properly. The Monoblocs that came with this bike had some wear evident on the throttle slide, but not too much so I decided to reuse them – especially after finding out the cost of replacements! The other main wearing parts, the float needles, throttle needles and needle jets, were replaced. A decision on replacing any further parts was reserved until after the bike was running. The bodies of the carburettors were cleaned using proprietary carburettor cleaner, the jets were all checked that they were clear of obstruction, and the bodies were lightly polished using Solvol Autosol chrome cleaner to remove petrol staining, and the carburettors reassembled with a new set of gaskets, fibre washers and rubber O-rings. One thing to note with the Monobloc is not to put a gasket under the float needle seat (which sits under the fuel inlet banjo) – if you do, the float needle seat will be raised too high and the fuel will flood out of the

carburettor through the tickler as the float needle cannot shut off the fuel.

Initial setting up of the carburettors was done on the bench, with the air screws positioned one turn out and the throttle stops set to be not touching the slides. The needle jets were set on to position 3 as per the standard specification. Note that there are five positions or slots on the needle that allow the height of the needle to be adjusted by sliding the needle clip into the appropriate slot. These positions are numbered 1 to 5 in the literature relating to the carburettor, with position 1 being the top slot on the needle. As the carburettors are not 'handled' it is awkward to get at the adjusters (pilot jet and throttle stop) on the left-hand side. For initial setting the throttle stop screw was left out, so that it was not touching the slide, and the air screw was one and a half turns out. These settings are recommended as a good starting point for fine tuning.

Petrol Tank, Oil Tank and Side Panels

Petrol and Oil Tanks

The petrol tank that came with the bike was in primer. It should have been chromed, and the primer was removed to assess its suitability for repair and then rechroming. The chrome was not in good condition, and there were numerous small dents. The left-hand badge fixing had a rusted-in, headless screw.

Investigations into the cost of repairing, rechroming and then repainting came up with bills that exceeded the cost of buying a replacement reconditioned chromed tank or new glass-fibre tank. In addition, there was a risk that the tank would leak if removing the old chrome then repolishing the metal of the tank making it too thin.

In the end, I decided that as this was not an 'originality at all costs' restoration, a new glass-fibre Spitfire 5gal tank was the best option – and I have always liked its shape and styling. These were available from Burton Bike Bits at the time of writing (see the Suppliers section). Reproductions of the original equipment stick-on BSA tank badges and the tank front bracket were

As the restoration nears completion, the bike could be wheeled out. The oil tank was in good condition and was reused after a clean-up.

also purchased. Of course, should a suitable tank become available then it can be fitted to return the bike to its original state.

The oil tank was in good condition, and just needed a light clean-up, both inside and out. Its paintwork (all black) was sound, and even the rubber mounts that it came with were in good condition and reusable. The inside of the tank was cleared of loose rust and scale by putting a handful of old nuts in it, and then giving it a very thorough shaking. The debris and nuts were then emptied from the tank, the nuts cleaned up and the process repeated until the nuts came out as clean as they went in. Then the process was repeated a further couple of times with the nuts and white spirit, to wash out the inside of the tank.

Once completed, a bit of engine oil was sloshed around in the tank to protect its inside surfaces. The tank was then reinstalled in the freshly powder-coated frame. It then had to be taken out to allow the mudguard and tool tray to be fitted, as recounted above.

Side Panels

The side panels on a 1965 Lightning are glass-fibre, and the panels that came with the bike had at least two different coats of paint on them over what appears to be the original Red. The two cast alloy winged BSA badges, which fitted into recesses in these early type side panels, were of two different background colours – one silver, one gold. The Dzus fasteners on the frame for

Side panels were new, and already coloured to match the tank. Transfers came from the BSA Owners' Club, and were for a later version of the Lightning, but looked good.

the rear side panel fixings were present, but the front fixings and their mounting bar, which is bolted to the frame in front of the oil tank, were missing. A new mounting bar, with fittings, was sourced. Burton Bike Bits, the source of the glass-fibre Spitfire petrol tank, was also offering matching side panels, so I bought these new to avoid any colour matching problems. They cost about the same as having the old panels refurbished and painted. I decided to use the later type of side panels, without the indentation for the cast BSA wing badge, and put later 'Lightning Power' transfers from the BSA Owners' Club on them.

The transfers were of the water-slide type, and were applied by soaking them in warm water and sliding them into position on the side panels. Excess water and air under the transfers were removed using a damp cloth. It is important to remove any air bubbles before the transfer is dry. Once the transfer was dry, then a coat of varnish was applied both to protect the transfer from knocks and to waterproof it.

Humbrol clear gloss varnish, usually found in model shops, is ideal for this purpose.

Electrics, Lights and Switches

Rewiring

The wiring was basically useless and needed to be totally replaced. While wanting to keep the bike looking original, an upgrade of the electrics to 12V was essential for day to day practicality. However, the upgrade was designed to retain the twin switch and ammeter configuration on the headlamp. The new wiring was based on the later 1968 onwards BSA 12V system, and used the same colour coding. The main deviation from the later system was the retention of the ignition and light switches in the headlamp shell, the use of a modern rectifier/zener diode replacement unit and the use of Boyer Bransden electronic ignition.

While the new wiring loom was based on the later (1968) BSA wiring colours, it used the original 1965 lighting switch. I fitted a new key-operated ignition switch on the bottom of the headstock by making up a bracket which was fixed close to where the 1966 onwards models had it, but left the original ignition switch in the headlamp, albeit not connected. The wire used was modern automotive thin-wall type multi-strand copper wiring of 16.5amp or 25amp continuous carrying capacity, depending on what it was expected to do in the loom. The design of the loom and wiring runs was decided once the positioning of non-standard components such as the Podtronics regulator/rectifier and Boyer Bransden electronic ignition black box and coils had been determined.

The loom was built up using the bike itself as a jig – making sure that everything fitted, that there was enough slack around the headstock, and that nothing was rubbing or touching anything hot! Once the loom was laid out on the bike and the wires cut to length, suitable connectors were added. Bullet connectors were all soldered, spade connectors were crimped and soldered. As lengths of wire had connectors fixed on both ends, continuity checks were carried out to ensure there were no dry joints at the connectors or breaks in the wire itself. Once the individual elements of the loom were completed, self-amalgamating tape was used to bind common wires together and the completed loom was fixed to the frame using black plastic zip ties.

Headlamp and Tail Light

The chrome on the headlamp shell was heavily pitted, and was too far gone to be rechromed. In addition, there were several extra holes scattered about the back of the shell. The particular headlamp shell used on the 1965 Lightning housed the light and ignition switches and an ammeter. It was only used on the BSA A65 range by the early Lightning and Rocket (1964 to 1965 seasons only), but was also used by Velocette. It was replaced with a second-hand item, which was originally painted black and had never been chromed. This may have come from an A65 Rocket or possibly a Velo! The chrome on the headlamp rim had appeared to be beyond saving, but half an hour with some Solvol Autosol chrome polish brought it back and it looked good. The light lens and reflector were replaced with a modern Wipac Quadoptic Quartz Halogen unit, which slotted straight into the recovered rim and takes current standard halogen bulbs and should provide suitably bright lighting.

The tail lamp (a Lucas type 564) needed a lens and a clean-up before it could be pressed back into service. The cheapest way of doing this was to buy a pattern rear light unit, and use the lens in combination with the original unit's backplate.

Battery and Charging System

There was no charging system aside from an early, non-encapsulated three-wire 6V alternator. This was replaced with a new encapsulated, two-wire 12V version. The rotor was inspected to ensure that the centre was not coming unbonded from the outer magnets. Seeing if the rotor could support its own weight while being picked up with a spanner on each magnet in turn tested the strength of the magnets. The rotor passed both tests.

A solid-state 'Podtronics' black box was, on the recommendation of several sources, used to replace both the rectifier and the zener diode to provide a combined charging and regulating of the battery. This was fitted to the rear of the battery under the left-hand side panel, where it should get a bit of wind to assist cooling.

The battery carrier dictated the physical size of the battery that could be fitted. As the bike had Boyer Bransden electronic ignition a reasonable size was required. In my experience, British twins with a 7amp/hour battery and Boyer Bransden ignition system work well, so I wanted to get as near as possible to that capacity. The largest capacity battery that I could find to fit the early carrier was a 5amp/hour version. However, in practice this has not presented any problems and the electrical systems seems to be coping very well. A new ammeter was installed when testing revealed that the existing one registered only a 1amp discharge with the headlamp on – an obvious under-reading with a 60W headlamp bulb.

The Boyer Bransden electronic ignition system black box was fitted in front of the battery, close to the new twin 6V coils, which were wired up in parallel as the Boyer Bransden system required. This meant that both coils fired on each engine revolution, giving a 'spare spark' on the exhaust stroke. This in turn means that swapping the HT leads (an old trick to prevent a thief from starting a British twin) will have no effect as the bike will start quite happily! The coils were placed on a single made-up bracket behind the engine in front of the oil tank – the standard A65 pre oil-in-frame position. New HT leads were fitted, along with new 5,000ohm resistance NGK suppressor caps, again as required by the Boyer Bransden system.

Switches and Miscellaneous

Switchgear is relatively simple on the A65. The existing headlight-mounted switches for lights and ignition were retained, but only the lighting switch was connected up – the ignition switch was kept for appearance's sake, but the ignition was controlled by a new, later type of key-operated ignition switch mounted under the fork stem on a custom-made bracket.

The handlebars carry a replica Wipac Tricon switch – a circular chromed steel design that gave horn, dip/main and cut-out functions, which was a lot better integrated into the handlebar design than the clamp-on affairs used by other British manufacturers.

The cut-out function is not currently connected as it is simply an earth, and I do not know what effect it may have (if any) on the Boyer Bransden ignition system if I connected it to the live side of the coils. The wires from the handlebar switch were routed into the head-lamp, where they were connected up to the relevant light and horn feeds. The rear brake light switch utilized a pull-on pattern Japanese type, rather than the standard BSA rotary type.

This was mounted on the side panel bracket and a custom alloy bracket made up that bolted on to the rear brake pedal to give a straight pull to the switch via a spring.

The horn was mounted on the front engine mounting bolt, the standard position for the BSA unit twins. While it is vulnerable to road dirt in this position, it should be audible to other road users. A proprietary unit sourced at an auto jumble was used.

Starting-Up and Running

Once the bike has been completed, the best and sometimes most frustrating part of the whole restoration can be getting the bike started and running. There are several things to sort out at this stage, including the final fitting of the petrol tank and routing the fuel pipes so that they do not foul on anything hot – such as the engine.

Setting the timing was carried out statically, finding top dead centre and then setting the Boyer Bransden ignition sensor to the correct position related to the back plate according to the instructions supplied with the ignition. New spark plugs (NGK B8ES) were fitted – it is a false economy to fit old plugs in a rebuilt engine.

The motor did not start first kick, which was a

Drive side of the completed bike.

Timing side of the completed bike.

disappointment, but eventually it did burst into life. It was obvious that some fine tuning was required, as the bike refused to tick over. However, of more concern at this stage was to ensure that there was oil returning to the tank. Initially, despite priming the oil lines and the filter, there was no sign of any returning – although the level of oil in the tank did seem to be dropping, indicating that it was flowing into the engine. However, after a heart-stopping period and just as I was about to stop the engine to avoid any damage, a healthy flow of oil started to run back into the tank. This delay was probably due to the oil ways and oil pipes in the engine filling and the return side of the oil filter also needing to fill.

During this drama, the ammeter was showing a healthy charge rate, indicating that the Podtronics black box was working, and the engine ran quite happily with the lights on. Even with the lights on the ammeter indicated that the discharge was balanced at about 2,500rpm, with positive charge above that engine speed, again indicating that the electrics were operating correctly.

The first phase of fine tuning of the bike was carried out – the ignition was adjusted statically to be as close as possible to the required settings. Final adjustments would be carried out once the bike was on the road. The carburettors were balanced, and the tickover was sorted following the instructions for setting Amal Monoblocs in the manual, through the adjustment of the pilot jet settings. The initial limited test ride on private ground was terminated as the front end was bobbing up and down like a pogo stick, and the front brake was totally ineffective. The front wheel was removed and the glazed brake shoes roughed up. The wheel rim was checked to see if it was offset, and it turned out that the tyre was not properly seated. This was sorted by letting the air out and reseating the tyre on the rim, blowing it up to twice the recommended pressure, then letting the pressure back down while bouncing the tyre on the high spot. The bike was booked in for its MoT test that would enable it to be legally ridden on the road, which it passed first time. Then the final phase of fine tuning of the carburettors and timing could be carried out and properly tested by running the bike on the public roads.

Suppliers

In the completion of the restoration I used a number of suppliers, including my local bike shop, not-so local bike shops, mail-order suppliers and auto jumbles. The quality of spares and the service received ranged from good to bad. The suppliers which I recommend below provided good service and quality spares are listed below.

My local bike shop, Rockerbox, 31 The Street, Wrecclesham, nr Farnham, Surrey GU10 4QS, Telephone 01252 722973, run by Darrel Babkirk and Arthur Frearson, provided excellent service, reasonably priced new and used spares and mechanical expertise. Their knowledge of the mechanical side of the A50/A65 range is extensive (as indeed is their knowledge of the Triumph range), they have excellent stocks of spares and they can find and order even the most obscure parts. I cannot recommend them highly enough, and find each visit to them a pleasure, despite ending up spending at least twice what I intended to!

Another local bike shop used was Hart Motorcycle Services, of Redfields Stables, Redfields Lane, Church Crookham, Hampshire GU52 0RB, Telephone 01252 851037. While not stocking specific BSA spares, they do carry oil and general spares such as carburettor fittings, cable nipples, tyres, inner tubes and so on. They also do number plates and MoT tests.

Burton Bike Bits, 136–138 Waterloo Street, Burton-on-Trent, Staffordshire DE14 2NF, Telephone 01283 534130, provided me with a large proportion of the spares I needed using both their over-the-counter service and mail order. They have taken the commitment to remanufacture hard to obtain parts, and I was particularly pleased with the new Spitfire tank and the remanufactured chrome mudguards that I bought from them. Again, like Darrel and Arthur at Rockerbox, the staff were a mine of information on BSA parts and were particularly knowledgeable about the subtle differences between various versions of the A65! Service was excellent, with spares being despatched when they said they would be, and arriving promptly and well packed, avoiding any damage in transit.

Kidderminster Motorcycles, 60–62 Blackwell Street, Kidderminster, Worcestershire DY10 2EE, Telephone 01562 66679, attend many auto jumbles and provide a postal service. Spares provided included various odds and ends, and most importantly new clutch and brake cables for the bike which fitted perfectly. Again, a helpful and quick service was provided.

Vehicle Wiring Products, 9 Buxton Court, Manners Industrial Estate, Ilkeston, Derbyshire DE7 8EF, Telephone 0115 9305454, provided a range of electrical components, including wires, connectors, ignition switch, Tricon handlebar switch and headlamp. Again, service was prompt and prices were reasonable.

In the US, parts are supplied by British Only Motorcycles And Parts, Inc., 32451 Park Lane, Garden City, Michigan 48135, Telephone 734 421 0303, email info@britishonly.com, website www.britishonly.com.

Bibliography

Bacon, Roy, *BSA A50/A65 Twins All Models 1962 – 1972* (Niton Publishing, 1990, ISBN 1 855 79001 7)

With the exception of the *Brooklands BSA Twins* this is the only book dedicated to the BSA unit twins. One of the Motorcycle Monograph range, it is a good but short book on the twins.

Bacon, Roy, *BSA Buyer's Guide* (Niton Publishing, 1990, ISBN 0 951 42041 0)

This contains a useful chapter on the unit twins. Also details engine and frame number prefixes and other range-specific details.

Bacon, Roy, *BSA Twins and Triples* (Niton Publishing, 1995, ISBN 1 855 79029 7)

Excellent history of the BSA twins and triples – another invaluable source for information on the range.

Bacon, Roy, *BSA Twin Restoration* (Niton Publishing, 2000, ISBN 1 855 79042 4)

Contains many original works photos and illustrations, but is rather mixed up between the individual models in the A7/A10 and A50/A65 ranges, so it can be hard to concentrate on a single model.

Clarke, R. M. *BSA Twins A50 & A65 Gold Portfolio*, Brooklands Books, Undated, ISBN 1 855 20337 5)

Compilation of contemporary road tests of BSA A-Series twins from the UK and US.

Holliday, Bob, *The Story of BSA Motor Cycles* (Patrick Stephens Ltd, 1978, ISBN 0 850 59277 1)

now out of print. Good history of the BSA motor cycles. It tends to concentrate more on the models up to the 1950s.

Hopwood, Bert, *Whatever Happened to the British Motorcycle Industry?* (Haynes Publishing, 1998, ISBN 1 859 60427 7)

The definitive account of the British motorcycle industry from the author's experiences of working for most of the major manufacturers, including BSA, from the 1930s through to the 1970s.

Ryderson, Barry, *The Giants of Small Heath* (Haynes Publishing Group, 1980, ISBN 0 854 29255 1)

Now out of print, but a complete history of BSA from its formation to demise.

Vanhouse, Norman, *BSA Competition History* (Haynes Publishing Group, 1998, ISBN 1 859 60430 7)

The book provides a detailed account of BSA's competition success and failures from the start of motor cycle production to the 1970 Triples.

Wilson, Steve, *BSA Motor Cycles since 1950* (Patrick Stephens Ltd, 1997, ISBN 1 852 60572 3)

This is a reprint of the BSA section of Wilson's six-part *British Motorcycles Since 1950*, and is a valuable reference source, as well as being a good read.

Wright, Owen, *BSA The Complete Story* (The Crowood Press, 1992, ISBN 1 86126 064 4)
This volume is a good, comprehensive history of BSA from its formation in 1855 to the end in the 1970s.

Sundry BSA literature, such as brochures and workshop manuals, are available through specialized booksellers and auto-jumble traders. Photocopies of parts books and workshop manuals are available from Bruce Main Smith & Company (BMS), and other vendors are also producing CDs containing scanned-in copies of original BSA factory manuals.

Index

Amal Concentric 75, 77
Amal Grand Prix 75, 77, 78, 116, 120
Amal Monobloc 75–77, 166
American Motorcycle Association (AMA) 116, 121
Anderson, Lindsay 59

BMW 94
Boddice, Mick 121
Bond, James 59
Brown, Peter 121
BSA history 5
BSA models
    3½ HP model 5, 112
    A7 7, 10, 70
    A10 7, 10, 70
    A10 Super Rocket 8
    A50 Cyclone 19, 24, 26, 27, 62, 120
    A50 Cyclone Competition 19, 24
    A50 Cyclone Clubman 24, 27, 28, 39
    A50 Royal Star 19, 21
    A50 Star Twin 10, 19, 20, 62
    A50 Wasp 19, 27–29
    A65 Firebird 55, 56–60, 62, 135–139
    A65 Hornet 48–52
    A65 Lightning 30, 34–44, 62, 139–146
    A65 Lightning Clubman 38, 39
    A65 Lightning Rocket 30, 34
    A65 Rocket 32, 34, 36, 37, 62
    A65 Royal Star 30, 62
    A65 Spitfire 44–48, 62
    A65 Spitfire Hornet 49, 62
    A65 Star Twin 9, 10, 30, 62, 131–135
    A65 Thunderbolt 30, 51, 52–56, 62
    A65 Thunderbolt Rocket 30
    A70 Lightning 57, 60–61, 65
    B50 61

    C15 113
    Gold Star 34, 87, 112
    Rocket 3 48, 116
    T65 Thunderbolt 60–61
BSA Owner's Club 168
Burrell, Chris 135–139

Cooper, John 'Moon Eyes' 114–115
crankshaft 67
Currie, Bob 7

Daytona Beach Races 75, 112, 116
Devimead 75, 123, 126

Ekins, Bud 59
Elmore, Buddy 120
Elphick, Michael 59

Fearon, Bob 7
French Grand Prix (1913) 112

Gould, Ron 121
Gunter, Al 121

Hailwood, Mike 115
Hanks, Norman 119, 121
Harris, John 113
Harris, Les 84
Holden, Ken 112
Hutchinson 100 Race 115

ISDT 113
Isle of Man TT 33, 112, 121

Kefford, Barry 121
Krukowski, Pete 119

Lucas 9, 10, 41, 48, 100–104, 107, 125

Mallory Park 121
Mann, Dick 121
Mason, Les 75
McGahan, Chris 119
Meriden 84

Nicholas, Jody 121
Nixon, Gary 120, 121
Norton 5, 7, 48, 93, 124, 165

oil-in-frame 44, 56, 59, 82, 85

Perrigo, Bert 8, 120

RockerBox 125, 171

Scott, Jeremy 131–135
Sheldon, Stan 91
Smith, Jeff 112
Smith, Tony 114, 116
Smiths (Instruments) 108–110
SRM 75

Tanner, Sammy 121
Thompson, Hunter S 30
Tribsa 66
Triton 66
Triumph 5, 122
    B-Series Twins (Unit 650) 15, 67, 69, 74
    C-Series Twins 15
    Model 21 (3TA) 7
    T110 15
    T120 Bonneville 68
    Thunderbird 15
    TR5MX 61

Umberslade Hall 56, 82

Vale, Nick 139–145
Vincent, Chris 118, 120–121
Vinicombe, Terry 116, 118

Winters, Robert 117
Wipac 105